Mountains Along Our Path

Betsy Campbell • Cleo Simon
Nancy Humphrey • Nancy Fetzer
Laurie Chandley

HALLARD PRESS

Published by Hallard Press LLC
www.HallardPress.com
Info@HallardPress.com

Bulk copies of this book may be obtained by contacting Info@HallardPress,com

Cover Design: Betsy Campbell
Page Design & Typography: Hallard Press LLC / John W Prince

Printed in the United States of America

ISBN: 978-1-951188-14-6

01

Dedication

This book is dedicated to

Maurene Miller (Womanwithspirit)
and
Doris Graham (Dustcatcher)

We remember that you lived and that your lives gave us
memories too beautiful to forget.

Prologue

The Gathering of the Hikers

Four friends got together in 1992 and took a trip to New England. They toured historic Boston and hiked through the beautiful mountains of New Hampshire. It was an invigorating and fun way to see the area and all agreed that they would like to do more hiking. All had the same adventurous spirit. Each year thereafter another trip was planned with mountain hiking at its core. It became a yearly event with the only unknown factor being where it would take place and who would be able to make it.

Every year a new destination was chosen, and each trip consisted of at least four to five women. Those who could make it made their plans to meet in the designated place. We soon dubbed ourselves the Happy Hikers. Through the 27 years of hiking together, we added trail names, pink hats and matching colorful T-shirts. This became our hiking attire.

No membership required here. We are just a group of friends who have a common appreciation for mountains vistas, a deep respect of nature, and relaxing camaraderie.

We first began to write notes of our trips and then the idea was proposed of writing a book about our experiences. Each Happy Hiker contributed their memories for a few chapters and we compiled it in this book. With any luck, it just might inspire someone else to put on their hiking boots and make their own wonderful times out in the great outdoors. Hope to see you on the trail.

The Happy Hikers

Betsy Campbell
Cleo Simon
Nancy Humphrey
Nancy Fetzer
Laurie Chandley

Table of Contents

Chapter One

The Beginning—1992

Boston, Massachusetts
White Mountain National Forest, New
Hampshire
Ogunquit, Maine

by Betsy Campbell, AKA Cloudsplitter

The whole adventure started with Cleo Simon. Cleo and her husband, Ed, owned the tennis club Rio Paz in Punta Gorda, Florida. I had recently moved from New Hampshire to a town just over the river from Punta Gorda.

After looking in the phone book for local tennis clubs that I could join, my eyes landed on Rio Paz Tennis Center. Still, I called another club first, but the line was busy. Skipping over a few others, I dialed Rio Paz's number. Ed answered and was most inviting. He lined something up for the next morning and told me it was just over the river past the farm store. *A farm store,* I thought to myself, *well that sounded wonderful!* I envisioned an open-air farm stand with lovely fresh Florida produce. Sounded great! In reality, Rio Paz was 21 miles from my house, and the farm store turned out to be a "Farm Store." It was a run-down convenience store in the middle of nowhere.

Rio Paz Tennis Center made up for any disappointment the Farm Store caused. Ed paired people with players of the same level so worrying about a partner was never a problem. All I had to do was show up and I could play the mornings or afternoons away. It was here that I met his lovely wife, Cleo. Soon, I was playing five days a week and had met many nice people.

There were four courts at Rio Paz and the better players were on 1 and 2 which was in one section. Most of the members on those two courts were the ones that I knew best. Cleo happened to play there, too.

Eventually, some of the beginners from courts 3 and 4 worked their way up to 1 and 2, so there was a rotation of sorts. One of the ladies that made it to court 1 was Nancy Humphrey. Cleo, Nancy, and I were soon playing frequently together.

After the members were done with their games, they could sit under a covered open-air patio, relax and visit. That was a perfect way to cool down and get to know each other better. Turns out that Nancy and Cleo taught school in the Desoto

County school system for many years. They had much to talk about, and I got to know them well through listening to their conversations. It was nearing fall when they were discussing flying up to North Carolina to visit Cleo's sister, Maurene, and see the foliage. I was headed the following month to New Hampshire for the same reason, so I could appreciate their upcoming trip.

While relaxing after tennis, they relayed their tale of another trip they had done in 1985. Cleo had found tickets to Cancun for 4 days and 3 nights, including airfare, for only $135.00 per person. Nancy, who was always ready to take advantage of a good deal, was happy to go along. Unfortunately, they had to drive three hours to Miami to catch their flight.

After arriving in Cancun, they decided to take a boat to another island to do some snorkeling. The boat was $30.00 per person which they felt was way too expensive, so they found a boat that transported the local people for only $2.00 each (which they thought was great). They arrived at the port to find a boat that should have held 40 people, but was carrying about 200.

Cleo looked at Nancy and said, "I hope you are a good swimmer." They did make it over and back on that boat without anyone falling off, not that it couldn't have happened at any time as there were people, children, and chickens squeezed in everywhere, even on the outside of the railing.

Another side trip they took while in Cancun was to see the Tulum Mayan ruins. They again caught the bus for the local people which took hours on a crowded, dusty, and bumpy road.

They arrived back in Cancun tired, very thirsty, but with a great adventure under their belts.

Of course, while traveling in foreign countries, one must be very careful about drinking the water. In spite of being extremely careful, Nancy was attacked by a grueling bout of Montezuma's revenge. It took her 3 weeks and $200.00 for medicine to get back to normal. Meanwhile, Cleo had been guzzling Pepto-Bismol in hopes that she wouldn't get the same malady. The Pepto worked! Still, years later they were fondly remembering the upbeat moments despite the minor setbacks.

Hmmm, I was thinking, *it just might be fun to travel with these gals.*

But it wasn't until we all were back from our northern visits, and were again sitting around after tennis discussing our different adventures that Cleo said, "Gee, Betsy, if we had known that you liked to travel we would have asked you to join us." It was too late for foliage anywhere at that time of year, but we did plan a trip the following summer to Boston and New Hampshire.

Cleo, mild mannered, is a petite blond who hails from Minnesota and stands 5'1". Please don't mistake her stature for any type of pushover on the tennis court. *Au contraire*—she is definitely a dynamo who gives her opponents a run for their money, and she wears a very long belt with notches in it. After all—all is fair in love and tennis.

Up and coming Nancy is taller than a lot of woman at 5'10". She is a brunette and her height helps her achieve superior reach on the tennis court. (Just try to get a tennis ball past her). She is a natural born athlete who has played most sports at one time or another. Growing up with four brothers helped, too. Her abilities on any court helped her gain quick ascension to court 1. One minute I did not know her, the next she was my partner. Lucky me!

So, we spent my first warm, beautiful winter in Florida playing tennis, riding bikes, exploring state parks, and getting to know each other better. As school teachers, Nancy and Cleo had their summers off. Cleo stayed in Florida most of the summer, while Nancy flew back to Illinois for several weeks to spend time with her family.

My husband and I still had a house in New Hampshire, and we spent as much time as possible there in the summers. That is where I was when Nancy, Cleo, and Cleo's sister, Maurene, flew into Boston's Logan Airport on July 30, 1992.

One thing I didn't mention to the girls is that I am a complete and utter chicken when it comes to city driving. Why alarm them? And so, at 5:00 p.m., I was waiting for them at Arrivals in my sister, Nancy's, Jetta. (I am sure they were glad I didn't arrive in my pickup). After the arduous drive from New Hampshire into the city and through the Callahan Tunnel, I greeted them with a confident face. Unfortunately, we had to drive back through the tunnel to get to downtown.

Cleo and Nancy could not believe the chaos, the honking, the terror on everyone's face (or was that mine?) At each light, hawkers lined both sides of the road selling food, drinks, souvenirs and religious prayer beads. Cleo said, "I think those beads are rosaries." She sat back looking out the window and added, "No wonder!" Ten lanes had to shrink down to two at the tunnel, or at least it seemed like it.

I yelled, "Inhale girls, we are going through!" We made it and I drove them directly to the Parker House Hotel. I was thrilled when the valet drove our car away.

The Parker House first opened in 1855. It has seen many notable guests aside from the four of us. Some of the more prominent lodgers were Dickens, Longfellow, Emerson and John Wilkes Booth, just days before Lincoln's assassination. Two notables that had worked there are Ho Chi Minh and Malcolm X. The hotel is steeped in history and a great location for touring downtown Boston.

Boston is an old city that didn't have planned roads back when horses were the mode of travel. The city just grew here, there, and everywhere. The roads were stuck in wherever they could fit them. This led to a chaotic layout for today's drivers who appear fearless and aggressive, probably out of necessity. So, ditching the car was a wonderful idea. The plan was to tour historic Boston on foot until it was time to leave for New Hampshire.

The best part about staying at the Parker House was the red lined Freedom Trail right outside the front door. We spent the rest of the afternoon and early evening exploring the wonderful historic sites on foot that were in the general vicinity of the hotel. King's Chapel and Granary Burial Ground were just west of the hotel entrance where Paul Revere, John Hancock, Samuel Adams, and John Adams are buried.

Next, we headed west to Boston Commons, Old South

Meeting House, and the State House. Later, we walked to the Union Oyster House for supper. We didn't have reservations, so we had over an hour wait. Even still, it was worth the wait and the meal was delicious. With full bellies, we wandered back to the hotel via Quincy Market and Faneuil Hall under the beautiful city lights.

Boston, after dark, was quite lovely compared to the hustle and bustle of day time. The air was cool, the noises diminished, and the many lights made it seem like twilight all night long.

This was the first time I met Maurene. If I hadn't known that she was Cleo's sister, I am not sure I would have guessed they were related. Whereas Cleo is thin and petite, in contrast, Maurene is taller and full-bodied. The blond hair should have tipped me off, but within the next hour while watching them interact, I knew they were sisters.

Maurene took in everything around her with interest, but without the surprise and shock of the rest of us. She was a real estate agent and completely comfortable with everything that happened. Super gregarious, she was perfectly at ease with meeting and talking to people. You could tell she was thoroughly enjoying the new adventures.

The next morning after breakfast we hiked more of the Freedom Trail, this time heading east. There was no end to the wonderful sites to see and super food to eat. Boston had the most delicious food. We toured the Old North Church, the Paul Revere House, Old State House, and the USS Constitution and many other historic sites. As we walked, Cleo and Maurene said they felt as though the signers of the Declaration of Independence were leading them on, willing to share their stories one more time.

Cleo's favorite was the Old North Church. We all had heard so many times "one if by land, two if by sea" but for her to be standing in the church looking up at the very window that held the signal lantern, and imagining Paul Revere racing through the streets was just pure and simple joy. We were thrilled, proud and humbled to be where so much greatness in America had begun.

But, while in Boston we felt it was only right to break with the reverie and go to the top of the Prudential Building. The quickest way seemed to be the city subway, the MBTA. We studied the city map and the map of the subway's blue, red, and green lines and had a general idea of where we were going.

Nancy is the champion map reader and led us in the right direction. We got on the train and watched as more and more people got in with every stop. As they were packing in and jostling with the movement of the train, Cleo literally disappeared from my view. She said she felt like she was being suffocated with all the taller people around her.

Luckily, she had a death grip on one of the poles as well as Nancy's belt. Nancy was trying to keep a close eye on her. As the train loaded and unloaded, Cleo had small reprieves. Finally, we arrived at our stop and once again got out into the fresh air surrounded by all of Boston's wonderful history. Cleo breathed a sigh of relief. Maurene was unfazed. Nancy and I were glad to be off the train. The rest of the day was spent seeing the view from the top of the Prudential Building and making our way back to the Parker House on foot.

Later, when the valet brought our car around I nervously headed out into the rush hour traffic once again. When we made it to the New Hampshire border, Cleo said, "Gee, Betsy, if we had known the traffic in Boston was so bad we would never have asked you to pick us up there."

I said, "Where else would you have flown into?"

Cleo said, "Anywhere else."

With big city experience under our belts, we headed to my house in Greenfield, New Hampshire to spend the evening. We stopped for supper in Wilton, New Hampshire at The Olde Wilton Diner. This fantastic diner was owned and operated by a little elderly lady that did most of the cooking.

We are talking real mashed potatoes with real butter and baked goods. We could see her cooking away while we sat at the counter waiting for her delicious food. Without a doubt, she made the best banana cream pie in the world. Sadly, she died a few years later and her wonderful diner ceased to be. But that night we feasted, and it did rival Boston's yummy food.

The next morning, we headed for the White Mountains stopping in Canterbury to have lunch and a tour of the Canterbury Shaker Village. This pristine settlement was established in 1792 by the Shaker sect, but is now functioning as a producing museum. We toured the buildings in which they are still making the famous Shaker furniture in the same old fashioned way. The gardens were bountiful, and the livestock were healthy and content looking. We only hoped their buddies weren't going to be served for lunch.

When it was time to eat, however, we sat down to a mostly vegetarian meal. No one looked recognizable, thank goodness. Our dinner started with a salad of many unfamiliar greens. Maurene said, "It sure looks like grass, but it tastes great." Everything was delicious and grown at the village.

On the way to Mount Washington via Franconia Notch, we stopped at the usual tourist attractions including the Old Man of the Mountain, (who back then, was still there), and the Flumes. We drove by Clark's Trading Post and their trained black bears without stopping because of all the cars in the parking lot. I have never seen Clark's Trading Post because even as a child my parents said it was too busy to stop. Here I am all grown up and I am thinking it is too busy to stop. Some things are not meant to be seen, even in a lifetime.

We walked around the grand Washington hotel, Bretton Woods, and took pictures of Mount Washington in the distant mist. We took the Tramway up to the top of 4,100 foot tall Cannon Mountain and hiked around the top until it was time to go back down. We drove through Crawford Notch as we headed south enjoying the awesome beauty of the mountains. Seeing the White Mountains is a must do, and Crawford Notch and Franconia Notch make for a beautiful circle drive around the White Mountains.

I wanted the girls to see a little of the Maine coast, so we drove north on scenic Route 1 to Ogunquit stopping briefly in Kittery and walking a beach trail. The Maine coast in the summer is massively crowded with tourists as it is Maine's finest season. It was a perfect summer day there which equates to slightly chilly by Florida standards.

We headed to the beach to test the Atlantic waters. No one had packed swimming suits, so wading sounded good. The air by the water was brisk enough, so we didn't even entertain the idea of taking anything more off than our shoes and socks. The ocean was excruciatingly cold although there were some around us that seemed unaware of this fact. We did manage to wade all the way up to our ankles.

The water was a numbing and a painfully cold 43 degrees. After a few quick pictures, we got dressed. Shoes and socks can really warm up a body. That was our extent of swimming in the North Atlantic Ocean.

Once we warmed up, we headed to town for food and a place to stay. The stores, sidewalks, and restaurants were packed with people. We managed to get something to eat, but getting a room proved to be an arduous task, so we drove out of town noticing for the first time that all the hotels and motels had "no vacancy" signs. After many miles we found one that said "vacancy." Eureka! It looked very promising.

It was an old two-story clapboard house up a short hill off the busy road. Unbelievably, there weren't any other cars. We went to the office and inquired about a room and price. The price for the four of us was just right—cheap. As the place was a little run down and needing a coat or two of paint, Cleo asked if we could see the room.

The attendant, a tall gaunt man, and I might add, a little odd, got the key and took us around to the back of the building where the rooms were. There was a clothes line filled with washcloths, towels, sheets, and pillow cases gently blowing in the summer breeze. (Anyone could have dryer troubles, right?)

As we walked by the clothes line, it was hard to tell whether the items had been washed recently or were just airing out. (Perish the thought). Nevertheless, the alarm meter began to hum for me, and I was hoping the girls were having some humming, too.

He unlocked the door to the room, and it was large and furnished with a double bed and two singles. He informed us that the motel was his place and run by him. Nancy sat on one of the single beds, and the iron springs squeaked under her and went down a good eight inches.

I tried one with the same results. Obviously, these were original beds, and on closer examination, all the mattresses were on bare metal springs. And, I noted, there wasn't any phone. And, only one way in or out. And, he had a key. AND, we were all alone.

The alarm meter was getting stronger along with a feeling of panic. I could tell by Nancy's face that this wasn't getting it for her either. While Cleo was talking to the proprietor, Nancy and I decided it was a no go. (After all, churches do have pews.) We gave Cleo and Maurene the "we are going" sign and headed out the door towards the car. Maurene was close behind us and ever polite Cleo was still making conversation with the owner.

The man said, "Don't go," as Cleo headed towards us.

"We are just going to look around," replied Cleo.

"You won't find anything else at this price," the man said.

"Well, we'll just see. We may be back," Cleo said as she got close to her fleeing companions.

"If you go now, you won't come back," he yelled to Cleo's back.

She turned around and politely said, "We may."

"Get in the car, Cleo," Nancy yelled. Just as Cleo made it in and locked the door, another hapless couple drove in looking for a room. Therefore, we were saved from his further badgering.

Relief ran through the car and after the cortisol rush died down, we could even see the fun and humor of the situation from the safety of the car. We drove several more miles down the road checking each motel for a vacancy and we finally found one that was quite pricey.

Once inside, we all felt it was worth the price. Cleo said, "It sure is better than Bates Motel." None of us knew the name of the motel on the hill, but we all knew what Cleo was talking about.

"Say," said Cleo, "in the future let's get our motels ahead of time so we don't have to do any frantic searching." We all agreed.

The next day we headed back to Massachusetts a little sad as our time together was up. There was, however, one last uneasy detail and that was the drive once again through Boston to the airport. We were on a one-way section of the highway near the Massachusetts border when suddenly there was a car coming straight towards us in the same lane.

Nancy, who was in the passenger seat said, "Hey, he's going the wrong way." He was flying towards us and at the last second, I swerved off to the left shoulder while the other driver drove right on by. He was oblivious that he was going the wrong way. Cleo and Maurene, in the back seat, were chatting happily. The sisters had missed the whole near-death episode. Impressive maneuvering on my part, my ego said, but I knew we had just gotten lucky.

After that, Nancy and I took a few deep breaths. We calmed down with Boston still ahead of us. As we squeezed through Callahan Tunnel, I could see Cleo's eyes widen in the back seat. Maurene was used to traffic and was just enjoying the ride. We arrived at the airport on time and in good shape. We said our final goodbyes, and I headed to the New Hampshire border.

Well, I was right about one thing, those girls are fun to travel with, if not downright dangerous.

Once I made it into the Granite State, I breathed a sigh of relief and made a mental note to never, ever, pick up or drop off anyone at Logan Airport again.

Chapter Two

Glacier National Park, Montana—1993

by Betsy Campbell, AKA Cloudsplitter

Had we known before hand how truly magnificent Glacier National Park was, we might have thought about saving it for later. Fortunately we didn't, and we got to experience its wonders and beauty while we were all relatively young. Or, I should say, at least much younger than we are today.

But, as we all know, life is uncertain at best, so why wait?

As with our previous trip, it was mostly an unknown before we arrived, other than what we read or talked about with others. You can be sure, though, that all our rooms were booked ahead of time!

In July 1993, Nancy, Cleo, Maurene and I boarded our respective planes to Kalispell, Montana, from our different locales. As it was summer, Nancy was coming from Illinois, Cleo from Florida, Maurene from South Carolina and I was coming from New Hampshire. We all met in Salt Lake City, Utah.

Nancy was in a frenzy of excitement and anticipation and it was hard to keep her calm for the journey still to go. Cleo had spent the last six months recuperating from a car accident, so this trip was her motivation to improve her strength and stamina.

The idea of climbing among snow covered mountains was thrilling and it would be a whole new adventure for her. I was a little frantic about leaving my animals in the care of their sitter, as always. (Did I mention that it included a dog, cats, chickens and a pig?) Fortunately for us, Maurene was her usual calm, collected, level headed self, ready for whatever fun was in store.

After we boarded in Salt Lake City, we overheard a few people talking about Montana. They were a few seats in front of us and it was difficult to hear. One of the ladies lived in Montana. She had been to Glacier National Park 18 times. She was talking to the people behind her about Glacier.

Apparently, there were quite a few of us on board that were first time visitors. Once we reached cruising altitude, the Montanan eventually unsnapped her seat belt and knelt on her seat backwards facing her audience. She filled in everyone listening on the wonders of Montana, especially Glacier National Park where we were headed. It was like a professor lecturing her students and we were taking notes. The lady made the park sound breathtaking and we were not alone in our rising excitement. Even the part about grizzlies sounded like an addition to our upcoming adventure.

The night before I flew out my dog, Rex, who must have felt the impending separation, chewed my glasses, not only crinkling the frames down to the wire inside, but he broke one of the lens. It was a completely thorough job. (Bad boy, Rex)

Once we landed in Kalispell, we got our rental car and drove to the Kalispell Mall to find an optical store. While waiting for the glasses, we toured the Charles Conrad Mansion in Kalispell. Charles Conrad was an enterprising man from Virginia who moved west with his brother and made his money in cattle, mercantile, banking and mining. He eventually founded the city of Kalispell in 1891 and built his lovely mansion. We had to thank the rascally Rex for the very interesting side adventure. (Good boy, Rex)

After we got my glasses, we drove to the entrance of Glacier National Park where we had a room at the West Glacier Highland Resort. As you know, all rooms were booked ahead of time per Cleo's great suggestion. This one just happened to be right beside an Amtrak station which might have had something to do with the super rates. Even booking ahead didn't prevent a little oversight like this. However, it did look cozy and comfortable.

We drove into the park and got information at the Apgar Visitor Center to take back to the motel as everyone was tired from the travel and time change. We were all looking forward to a good night's rest. Nancy and I were having a hard time settling down and kept chatting about what we wanted to do. We were interrupted by the directive, "Lights out girls," issued by Cleo. Well, that certainly wasn't anything that I had heard in years, but we knew what it meant.

Cleo had the right idea, but many times, which seemed like all night long, sleep was interrupted anyway by the roar of the train starting and stopping, loading and unloading its passengers.

"My, that's quite noisy," said Maurene out of the darkness. There was no sense feigning sleep. We were all awake, but Nancy and I didn't dare say a word.

Next morning dawned bright and sunny and the train was forgotten even though it was still picking up and dropping off people. We headed for breakfast in the hamlet of Apgar on the shores of crystal clear Lake MacDonald. The very first glimpse of Lake McDonald was almost heart stopping, and let us know that we had wonderful discoveries ahead of us. The pristine glacier lake was a gorgeous unreal turquoise. Huge mountains with snow covered tops back dropped the lake. There were wild flowers abounding. It completely took our breath away.

"This is a scene staged by God," breathed Cleo.

After a while our stomachs turned our attention to food. Just looking at the mountains made you want a big breakfast. Most likely we would have wanted one anyway, but we had a beautiful reason in front of us. Big mountains call for big appetites.

We decided to do the hike to Avalanche Lake on the 5 Mile Avalanche Lake Trail. We found ourselves surrounded by more beautiful tall mountains. The scenery was stunning in all directions and the day was lovely. There were many cascading waterfalls in the circle of mountains at Avalanche Lake. The lake was just as blue and clear as any glacier lake can be.

Being big waders, we took our boots and socks off and waded up to our calves. Amazingly, these glacial lakes were warmer then the Atlantic Ocean in Maine, but by no means was it warm. It was cold. At least, no one else was swimming, that we could see, so it made us feel less like wimps. The surrounding mountains were just breathtaking.

We stayed the next two nights at the Lake MacDonald Lodge which seemed like the most perfect place to stay in the park. Nestled on the shores of Lake MacDonald, this classic lodge was a hard place to leave. As it turned out, it is just one of many beautiful lodges.

Easily, we could have grabbed a rocking chair and stayed right there all day. A good book, lake view, whispering pines, it was all very tempting and inviting. We tore ourselves away from such thoughts and hiked the John's Lake Loop Trail and took a drive up to Polebridge along the park's western boundary.

The town of Polebridge was electric free and consisted of just a few buildings, one being the Polebridge Mercantile which was an all-purpose store that served great pastry. The bathroom was an outhouse in the back and as each of us found out, had been well used. No one spent any longer than necessary in there and when it was my turn (I was last) I heard a hornet buzzing and looked up and sure enough, there was a nest on the ceiling. I'm sure that the girls had riled them up, but I didn't want to be the one inflicted by the hornet's anger. Out I flew barely getting my pants up. And of course, Nancy was videotaping the outhouse not knowing how quickly I would exit.

"Gosh, there are hornets in there," I said.

"Sure there are Betsy," said Cleo, in her knowing way, thinking it was the fragrance that got to me.

"No, there really are!" Hornets or no hornets, no one was going back in there to see.

Nancy is the one who has the video camera and we rely on her to capture the action, outhouse action included. The rest of us had cameras, but Cleo is the Queen of Cameras. For some reason she always has challenges with her camera. Today's challenge was seeing which side was the front or back.

She was having trouble seeing through the view finder in the bright sun. She studied the front, then the back, looked again through the view finder, then back to the front with a perplexed look on her face. Then she looked back to the back and yes, even the bottom. The three of us were laughing away, and eventually she looked up from the camera not knowing we had been watching her. She laughed when she realized we were watching her antics and good naturedly said, "It's hard to see." Yup, Nancy caught it all on video.

We had reservations with the Great Northern Glacier Expedition for a raft trip down the Flat River with an overnight in a teepee. We checked in at the office and were all issued water jackets, pants, boots, and life preservers.

Fancying myself hardier then the others, I decided to forego the pants. This was even after Nancy asked, "Are you sure you don't want the pants?" Once on the raft and under way, I was the only one in cotton sweatpants. It didn't seem like too much of a problem until it was too late to do anything about it. Further down the river the water got rougher and kept splashing on us and into the boat. My pants soon were wet. It was freezing, and I quickly realized my mistake.

The young (and I might add good looking) pilot was tan and bare chested when we started and didn't seem to mind what was quickly becoming numbing cold water splashing on him. When we took off, Nancy and I were mesmerized watching the pilot's tanned muscles rippling stoke after stroke with each exertion.

The sun was setting low behind the trees. My pants were totally soaking wet, the air was chilly, and I was shivering. I no longer cared about the pilot's stupid muscles. I wanted off the boat.

I knew I was in trouble. I kept remembering that a person could have hypothermia in water at 50 degrees. This felt much colder. I put my feet in a bailing bucket that was on board just for the added warmth. Nancy leaned her back up against my back and the tiny bit of warmth through the rubber jackets helped a little. Cleo and Maurene were aware of my *faux pas* and sweetly didn't say peep about it as they were getting chilled themselves.

We were all cold and it was getting dark. Even our pilot put on his jacket. He kept saying just a little further. We were all hungry, cold (some freezing), when we finally landed on shore in the dark. There was a fire burning in the distance which was hopeful. Just getting out of the raft was warmer.

The camp host showed us to our teepee which was an honest to goodness real teepee. Well, it was made of cloth and not animal skins, but it looked real enough for us. There were four or five cots consisting of plywood and a foam mattress on large logs along the perimeter. Looked like home.

The girls removed their water wear except me who thankfully had a change of clothes. By flashlight, we picked our cots and spread out the sleeping bags, then we went out to the fire and supper. The fire felt so good and warmed up my whole body.

By campfire we had steak, salad and beans which was great and after some conversation went back to our teepee. The topic of grizzlies came up because there wasn't any door on the teepee, much less a lock. We closed the flap as best we could and tried to get some sleep. Even in our sleeping bags we needed winter caps and Maurene even had a scarf wrapped around her face. Before drifting off to sleep, we discussed the chances of a grizzly coming into our teepee.

Fortunately, there were a few other teepees to choose from. We figured the odds were pretty good that we would see daybreak and after all, a grizzly can only eat so much, right?

You would think that after the Polebridge outhouse any other outhouse would have been an improvement. When we saw the nice wood outhouse in the middle of the woods it looked swanky. Upon entering it, we were greeted by a nice wooden bench with nothing but a black plastic garbage bag underneath. It is an environmentally sound practice to pack in, pack out, but the idea of doing "it" in a plastic bag was bothersome, not to mention the sphincter slamming reflex it induced. We all managed to use it or hold it. Just another of life's lessons 101.

Morning broke crystal clear and sunny and we forgot about the cold, scary night. The fear of being eaten alive disappeared as we got our first glimpse of the teepee by day. It was beautiful. There were colorful painted Indian designs on it that we couldn't see the night before.

Through the low morning mist, we could see a few other teepees between the tall pole pines. After a hearty breakfast by the fire (and a last visit to the outhouse), we got back on the raft in the warmth of the sunshine. The water was still cold, but the sun warmed us, even partially drying my sweatpants. Everything looked better by daylight.

While we were eating breakfast that morning, some late risers emerged from their teepee. It was a group of women who obviously were late due to primping. All the ladies were dressed to the nines with jewelry, makeup and cute hairdos. (Like what's with that?) Apparently, no one told them they were just putting on the same old musty water gear and getting back on the raft, which they did, only looking much more glamorous and feminine then everyone else.

Maurene said, "I am sure that they are the cause of the

term "glamping." Well, we knew it wasn't us.

Back on the Flat River, we passed a camera crew filming along the shoreline. Our pilot informed us that they were filming the movie "The River Wild" starring Meryl Streep and Kevin Bacon.

That evening we stayed in the Lakeview Tourist Resort, another magnificent lodge, and studied the wonderful invention of the flush toilet. "Watch this," Nancy exclaimed, "you just push the handle." The flush toilet is definitely taken for granted, but that night it was revered and appreciated by all of us.

The next few days we spent hiking, armed with pepper spray, on the Many Glacier Trail and the Iceberg Trail, each of indescribable beauty. All the trails presented dramatic vistas with drop-offs, precipices and sheer beauty all around.

Beautiful alpine wild flowers dotted the scenery along with picas, marmots and Dall sheep. We could spot several mountain goats on the distant sheer cliffs. It seemed impossible that they could have any footing whatsoever.

When Cleo and Maurene arrived at the crystal clear turquoise water of Iceberg Lake, Maurene said, "Wow, I can't believe we are finally here at the spot that we have been taking pictures of all day. Wow!" Only now the picture was even more spectacular with the lake in front of the well photographed mountain and its snowy glaciers.

Cleo and Maurene wanted to stay longer, and enjoy the view so Nancy and I headed back. Cleo and Maurene nestled in among the flowers and just let all the loveliness delight them.

Naturally, they overstayed and still had five miles to go before dark. They had been warned by the park ranger to make noise to alert any bears in the area. One of the Glacier park rangers had told us, "Hiking without grizzlies is like kissing your sister."

We still didn't want to run into any grizzlies on any trail. So as they hiked they sang every song they knew, and Maurene knew lots of camp songs, the good oldies like, "You Are My Sunshine," and "On Top of Old Smoky." That was five miles of singing loudly, and shouting every joke they could remember. Their plan worked. They saw no bears!

Logan Pass at 6,680 feet was crowded with people, buses and cars. The trail that we were going to hike was closed due to grizzly danger, and although it didn't state "attack" we knew what it meant.

We opted to catch one of the many buses that would take us on the Going-to-the-Sun road, a 50-mile-long road that bisects the park. Besides, it sounded safer than a bear attack. However, the road trip itself was a thrilling and scary ride, especially in the park's high riding buses. It is a narrow road following the mountain's grade filled with hair pin turns and sheer drop-offs that made my stomach queasy. Maurene quietly said, "So, how unfriendly are the grizzly bears?"

I am the group's reservationist. I like to book rooms and cabins with character and charm as well as cheaply as possible. Sometimes it works, sometimes it doesn't, and up to this point the rooms had been top shelf. On the east side of the park, I booked a cabin in Babb for a few nights. Turns out it wasn't in the park, but it was cute and way out in the middle of nowhere.

All the land around it was flat and barren compared to what we had just left. Just down the road was a small convenience store and other than that it was quite desolate. It was just barely dusk when we got to the cabin. The inside of the cabin was small, but adequate other than there was only a partial wall between the bedrooms.

The overhead shelf in the bedrooms hung over the beds and you had to shut the bathroom door all the way to be able to sit on the john. Minor points when you consider the price. Hey, the toilet flushed.

The days of hiking must have tuckered Maurene out and no one there would ever deny that she didn't get the very best sleep that night. In the middle of the night Cleo, Nancy and I woke to a very loud noise that was emanating from Maurene herself. On and on the snoring went keeping everyone up but one. All agreed that it was due to that blasted partial wall acting as a sounding board!

In the middle of the night, Nancy had to get up to use the facilities. (Well, she was awake anyway.) Only in the dark, she cracked her head on the brace of the overhead shelf. That ensued a light being turned on, checking to make sure she was all right, and waiting until she was done before lights out again. With all the commotion, Maurene took a break from her snoring. Unfortunately, it was only a short break.

It wasn't until the next night, when we needed something down at the store, that we realized we were in Indian territory.

There were only Indians in the store and the store keeper, an Indian himself, informed us that we were on the Black Feet Indian Reservation. That was fine with us. It completed the wild west experience. None of us had ever spent a night on a reservation before.

Back in the park, we hiked Highline Trail, Many Glacier, Five Glacier, and Grinnell Glacier Trail over the next few days. On each hike, the silence was interrupted with someone shouting in the distance. You learn quickly that making noise alerts the grizzly bears that you are in their area. It would be nice to think that a peaceful and quiet hike would be in order, but self-preservation always wins out. The threat of grizzly even kept me, who usually wanders ahead of the pack, to stay close.

On the Highline Trail, which is quite crowded until you've gone out a few miles, we had to move off the trail to let a mom Dall sheep and her lamb go by. There was a standoff for a few seconds, but the sheep won. It's best to respect all the animals that live there.

We rounded out our trip by driving into Canada, destination the Prince of Wales Hotel. When we got to customs, we were asked if we had anything dangerous, aerosol, etc. Honest Cleo said she had some pepper spray which they had her get out of her suitcase. We were asked again and the rest of us said nothing. Like who wanted to give up their pepper spray in grizzly country other than Cleo? We finally got the go ahead.

As we pulled away, Cleo said, "Do you think we should have given them the rest of the pepper spray?"

Maurene replied, "Well, it's too late now." Then it was off to the Prince of Wales Hotel in Waterton, Canada with three cans of pepper spray.

The Prince of Wales is a majestic hotel sitting on a hill overlooking Waterton Lake and surrounded by the Canadian Rockies. Breathtaking doesn't quite describe it. The hotel was built in the 1920's and is stunning in its rustic presence. Waterton Lakes National Park begins where Glacier National Park leaves off. In 1932, the two parks were dedicated as Waterton-Glacier International Peace Park, marking a long era of good will.

A 20 foot swath through the forest identifies the boundary between the US and Canada. We took the Waterton boat back down the lake into Montana, crossing over the international line and stopping for a brief time at Goat Haunt, which is basically a wilderness ranger station that backpackers use as a jump off point.

As always, the ride to the airport in Kalispell was a sad reminder that a fun time was drawing to its end. Only this time Cleo and Maurene were leaving a day before Nancy and me. So, we said our good-byes to them, looked at each other, and said, "Now what?"

We discussed going back in the park, but ended up driving around Flathead Lake and checking out Big Fork. Before we knew it, it was the end of the day and we didn't have any place to stay. (Someone had fallen short of booking that last night.) We stopped in many places to see if we could get a room for the night, but all motels were full. We got supper and discussed sleeping on a church pew. Nancy had done that several times in college. Therefore, we tried a church in town, but the doors were locked. We discussed calling the police and seeing if they had any extra rooms. We tried one more hotel before that and they were booked full also, but the kind desk clerk gave us a list of motels, hotels and B&B's in the area. After many calls, at 10:30 p.m. we got a "Yes."

The bed and breakfast lodging was about 25 minutes out of town, but it sounded better than a jail cell, even one that you went to voluntarily. We headed up the dirt driveway in the dark and hoped that it wasn't another Bate's Motel. We were a bit apprehensive.

The friendly owner greeted us in the driveway and showed us by flashlight to our room. Only it wasn't a room, it was an apartment over a barn, and it wasn't a small apartment either. There were three bedrooms, full bath, laundry and kitchen. Fresh muffins and cherries were on the table and the refrigerator had milk, butter and fruit. Wow, it was great! After checking everything out, we picked our bedrooms and went to sleep.

We awoke to roosters crowing at dawn. From the kitchen we were greeted to another beautiful clear big sky day with gorgeous mountain views. Nancy videotaped our lovely accommodations to show the girls. Vowing to come back to this great spot again, we said good bye to our sweet hosts and drove to Kalispell.

Nancy said, "What a way to end a great trip."

Chapter Three

Acadia National Park, Maine—1994

Mount Katahdin, Maine

Nancy Humphrey, AKA Thunderfoot

I was hoping this trip would start off with a bang, but instead it started off with a "pop." Maurene was not able to make the trip to Maine, so Cleo and I enlisted a fellow teacher friend of ours, Sue Valade, to join the group. Sue was more than happy to go to New England as her son, Mike, his wife and children lived in New Hampshire while he was attending Dartmouth College's

Radiology School.

Cleo's niece, Laurie, Maurene's daughter, lived and worked in Nashua, New Hampshire, so flying into Manchester gave Cleo and Sue the perfect opportunity to visit with some of their family.

On August 8, 1994, after a happy and fun visit with new friends and relatives, Cleo, Sue and I headed back to our motel for a good night's rest. We weren't asleep too long when the hotel fire alarm went off. We frantically got up and headed down the stairs to the outside.

The fire engines arrived with the sirens blaring and the lights flashing. Of course, we were scared until we got outside and discovered all the hullabaloo was because somebody had just burned some popcorn in a microwave making the fire alarm go off. "Pop, Pop, Pop!"

The next morning, Betsy met us for breakfast in Manchester and we headed up the coast of Maine on scenic Route 1. Our first stop was Kennebunkport. Since one of Cleo's rules was to always take the local trolley, which in this case was a horse drawn trolley, we went on a tour of Kennebunkport.

The driver gave us the history of the area, along with a look at the main sites in town. One of those sites being the summer home of former President George H. W. Bush. The trolley stopped so we could see the Bush Compound in the distance and we all got a glimpse of the "Silver Fox" out in the yard. Perhaps, at that distance, it could have been anyone with white hair, but we all agreed it was Barbara Bush, regardless.

As hikers, we are always looking for interesting hiking gear. Of course, we stopped in Freeport to see the L.L.Bean store. Freeport was store after store of wonderful things tantalizing the senses and wallet. The Maine coast was always crowded with tourists in the summer, but this shopping mecca was crawling with people. The checkout lines were very long which didn't seem to discourage anyone. We limited our time mainly to the L.L.Bean store, then continued along the coast to the Camden-Rockport area.

I had always loved the movie, *Andre*. Consequently, we went to Rockport Harbor to see that famous seal. Unfortunately, and unknown to us then, the harbor seal had died eight years previously. There were still signs telling about him. He lived more than 25 years and became an icon of Rockport.

The movie *Andre* was an adaptation of a book by Harry Goodridge. The book highlighted many of the tricks that the author taught Andre. In real life, Andre entertained crowds with jumping through hoops, shaking hands and giving the Bronx cheer. He even was the ring bearer at Goodridge's daughter's wedding. Goodridge took care of Andre from the time he was an orphaned pup, until the day that he buried him. There is now a granite statue of Andre overlooking the harbor that he lived in and loved.

We reached Acadia National Park near sunset and drove to the top of Cadillac Mountain to watch the sun go down. Then off to our cozy cabin and rest for the next busy day.

Morning brought chilly air as we walked the rocky shore

watching ships in the distance and many *pleine air* painters capturing the beautiful dramatic coast line. We checked out booming Thunder Hole. Thunder Hole was a small inlet, naturally carved out of the rocks. At the end of the inlet, down low, was a small cavern where, when the rush of the wave arrived, air and water was forced out like a clap of distant thunder. Water may spout as high as 40 feet with a thunderous roar! Hence the name: Thunder Hole.

Nearby, there was a group of tourists looking out over the ocean. We joined them with cameras ready. One lady was narrating the scene on the distant horizon where there appeared to be two whales. The lady said that it was a mother whale with her calf. As the waves rolled in they would disappear from sight, but soon came back into view. Click, click went the cameras. This was good stuff, though after about 10 minutes and 400 pictures later, the whales had not moved on the horizon. It turned out that the whales were two rocks in the water. Oh well, the tourists got their would be whale pictures!

Acadia National Park had several outstanding hikes. One was the Beehive Trail. It was considered strenuous and not recommended for people with a fear of heights. Good traction shoes were advised. The hike began on the Bowl Trail, but soon the Beehive Trail went off to the right. There was a sign warning of the danger of falling.

The first section of the Beehive had iron rungs to allow climbers to ascend exposed, steep cliff faces and traverse narrow ledges. After reaching the top, hikers were rewarded with outstanding views of Sand Beach, Great Head, and Frenchman's Bay. Cleo and Sue opted out of that trip.

Another family friendly and fun hike we took was to Bubble Rock. We began the hike at the Bubbles parking lot, and went to the Bubbles Divide trailhead. The climb was a well maintained trail that slowly ascended to the legendary 100 ton Bubble Rock.

Some people called it Balance Rock because it was on the edge of a cliff. We expected the rock to fall down the mountain at any time. Cleo tried to push Balance Rock over the cliff, but she hadn't eaten her Wheaties that morning—only oatmeal.

Just past Bubble Rock, we came to a view of Jordan Pond. This place gave us an awesome view for our lunch. After lunch, we continued down the South Bubble Trail. The farther we went, the bigger the rocks got. The trail worked its way through a forested boulder field. We didn't know how we would get through all those boulders, but slowly and surely we did.

After our boulder scrambling, we rewarded ourselves with an afternoon break of tea and popovers on the lawn of Jordan Pond House. Yummy!! The Jordan Pond House Restaurant, with views of Jordan Pond and surrounding mountains, had been serving popovers and jam since the 1890's.

We also did a four hour whale watching trip. I should never have gotten on that boat. It was four hours of seasickness. Bah humbug!! We did see several whales on that trip and the rest of the girls thought the water was nice and smooth. Bah humbug to them too!

From Acadia National Park, we headed to Baxter State Park

to climb the high point of Maine, Mt. Katahdin. Cleo and Sue were not joining us on that hike. This was our very first state high point. I had no idea of what we were getting ourselves into. The 18 mile trip from Millinocket took us an hour. Inside the park entrance, we stopped at the information center which took a half hour, but we did receive much needed information, such as making sure to get an early start! Another half hour was lost by the drive on the gravel road to our starting point. At 11:00 a.m., we began our 10 mile hike up and over Mt. Katahdin—a little too late and ill-prepared.

The first mile on the Hunt Trail, which follows the Appalachian Trail, was a gentle hike through the woods following the Katahdin Stream and it seemed like it was going to be an easy hike. Then the rocks and uphill climb started. I thought I was prepared for that.

Being a flatlander, I was not even close to being aerobically fit enough for that hike. To tell how bad it was, my hiking partner, Betsy, who was walking a few feet behind me, so I could set the pace, said to me, "What is that noise I hear?" I said, "I hate to tell you this, but it is my heart."

We then sat down and talked about whether or not we should continue. The decision was to go on, but very slowly, and stop if it happened again. What lay ahead of us were huge boulders 10 to 20 feet tall.

This was an ideal spot to turn around as it appeared to be the end of the trail. Again, these thoughts were gently roaming around our minds. We decided to go ahead. We had planned and talked about this trip for months. I didn't have the heart to tell Betsy that I couldn't continue. Betsy said, "Climb up and see how the trail looks so you will know if we should continue."

I climbed up, looked around at some of the rocks and said, "Oh! It doesn't look too bad!" I must have been nuts!

The going was very slow as we worked our way over the rocks. Paint marks and embedded iron pins were the only indication which way the trail went over the wall of rock. We would take off our packs. I boosted Betsy up, handed her the packs, then with my long legs I pushed myself up with her help.

We had to do that over and over. For the next three-quarters of a mile, the trail was nothing but big boulders that wound along the precipice of that slice of rock. The mountain had sheer drop-offs of over 1500 feet on either side.

This was the most exhilarating section of that trail. Betsy was trying to keep herself scrunched down and not look over the sides. I began to feel sick to my stomach, which made me feel weak all over. Betsy came over and began giving me words of encouragement. Like, "We have to get going or we won't get off the mountain before dark." It worked, for after a 15 minute rest we continued. We could just make out tiny figures of hikers ahead of us on what appeared to be the summit. This encouraged us to trudge on. I shouldn't say that. Betsy had never trudged in her life. Trudging was my style.

At about four miles, we crested the rock wall that we thought was the top. Before us was a flat section of alpine field that stretched out for a mile with the true summit in view. From everything we had read and seen about Katahdin before our trip, nothing had prepared us for the beautiful, level tableland that lay before us.

Delicate alpine flowers and plants were everywhere. At this point, it was like entering into another realm. It had the feel of another world. The day was sunny and clear and the world spread endlessly in all directions. A feeling of calm came over us and with renewed energy, we continued to the top.

There is always a special feeling that we have when we reach the top of a mountain, but this was definitely different. It is a humbling sensation to see how grand mountains are and this was breathtaking. How insignificant we seemed, yet so honored to be on such a spiritual place.

As much as we would have liked to spend more time at the top, it was already 4:30 p.m. when we arrived. It had taken us five hours to make the 4,168 foot elevation gain to the summit. In order to make it down before dark, we couldn't dillydally.

There was a German couple that arrived at the top while we were there. We wanted some video of us at the top and asked them to film us. This was an adventure all by itself. Explaining how to run a camera without being able to speak the same language was a challenge. We got a lot of film of the ground, the rocks and finally some of us on top of Katahdin.

We got only a glimpse of the mile long Knife Edge Trail renowned as the most spectacular trail in the east. At places, this trail was only four feet wide with 2,000 foot drops on either side creating a nearly technical route in places. We were warned to stay away from that trail in bad weather. Well, the weather was fine, but that would have to wait for another time.

Our all-cotton clothes were very wet from the climb and the wind was whipping at the top. In minutes, we were chilled, so we started down the Saddle Trail to Chimney Pond Campground. We were so happy to be heading downhill for a change, but the trail was narrow and consisted of small rocks, scree and talus. We literally had to sit down and slide a great deal of the way. We ran out of food and muscle cramps developed in my lower legs. I wanted to lie down and go to sleep or die, whichever came first.

When we finally reached Chimney Pond Campground, the sun was starting to go down. I spend my time between Florida and Illinois, both predominantly flat, so I was exhausted. We decided to knock on the Ranger's door. We asked if there were any camping spots available. He said, "No, they are all full."

So, we asked if we could sleep on his porch. He didn't think that was funny and had no mercy for us when he gave us his emphatic, "No!" He said, "You are in better shape than most that come down Mt. Katahdin."

He did soften to the point of reluctantly giving us a flashlight to be turned in at Roaring Brook Campground and radioed ahead that we were on our way. I was still in disbelief that we were being turned away, so I headed for one of the cabins and told Betsy that I was going to find someone friendly and bunk in with them. Betsy didn't go for that at all. I had to listen to those same words from Betsy, "We have to get going or we won't get off the mountain before dark."

The final two-and-one-half miles were still ahead and we made the best time we could in the semidarkness. Every muscle felt strained and sore. We took each step one by one and talked our way down as fast as our bodies could manage.

Finally, we got to a few segments of trail that were smooth. Betsy would yell, "Big step area!" Then, I knew I could try and make some time as twilight had settled in around us. Fortunately, the closer we got to Roaring Brook Campground, the better the trail became and the faster we went. Darkness was now upon us, but we would soon be united with Cleo and Sue. We walked the last 100 feet arm in arm with a smug feeling of great accomplishment and triumph.

There is something about Katahdin that makes it a special experience and calls us back. We learned many, many things about what to do and what not to do on this hike. The privilege of climbing Katahdin and basking in its austere beauty only left us wanting for more, and thus led to our goal of doing all the other high points of the United States, but Katahdin, we wait to do again.

Chapter Four

Alaska—1995

Denali National Park, Alaska
Kenai Fjords National Park, Alaska

Cleo Simon, AKA Runningbehind

Our trip to Glacier National Park was such a wonder to Nancy, Betsy and me that whenever we got together the following year, we always asked each other, "How can we ever top that trip?" On one of our Glacier reminiscing sessions, out of the blue, Betsy said, "Maybe Alaska?" Our eyes locked, adrenaline rushed and we knew this was it! Alaska, that far away state, Seward's Folly, mysterious Alaska, got us moving.

Since it would be a very expensive trip, we decided to go in two years. This would give us time to research, plan, and save pennies. I called Maurene in South Carolina and she was "in." The Glacier foursome was going to Alaska!

In 1995, we booked our flights six months early, but somehow we all got seats in the very back of the plane over the engines. It was a long, loud flight. We were determined that would not happen on the way back.

The first night in Anchorage, we stayed at Bonnie's Bed and Breakfast. That evening when we unpacked, Maurene found a love note from her husband, Bob, in her suitcase. We all thought that was special. Betsy and I were so jealous for nary a love note from our husbands was found tucked in our suitcases.

Later as we sat in bed and talked, Maurene told us she would not be able to do any climbing. She could only do flat trails. When we asked if anything was wrong, she said she just was not able to do that any longer. This totally puzzled me, because she led me on every hike two years earlier in Glacier and she was only seven years older than me. I thought, could Maurene get this much out of shape in two years? She seemed just the same; peppy, full of life, and ready for a laugh.

The next morning, we were up early, had a fantastic Alaskan (big) breakfast, and hopped into the car to catch the train from Portage to Whittier. The railway had been built in 1943 to transport soldiers from Anchorage to Whittier. During WWII the US Army constructed a military facility there. Whittier had no road access in 1995.

After we purchased our tickets, we were told to wait for the train on the deck of the depot platform. Nancy had all her gear in hand, backpack, fanny pack, camera bag, water bottle and ticket. It was an extremely windy day and suddenly a huge gust of wind swooped by us. We all watched frozen in place as the wind ripped Nancy's ticket out of her hand and swirled it perfectly down between the slats of the platform.

We all got down on our hands and knees to peer through the cracks to try and see it. Nancy spotted the ticket, but how do we get it? Maurene asked, "Anyone have some string and gum?" We didn't have long before departure so we had to do something quickly.

Our hero came in the form of a gentleman in his late teens. He and everyone on the deck noticed us kneeling and looking distraught. He crawled under the deck, grabbed the ticket and inched back out. We dusted him off, thanked him profusely and with that, everyone got on the train amid many smiles and chuckles.

We had a two hour scenic train ride from Portage to Whittier, known as "the town under one roof." In Whittier, the Begich Towers house about seventy-five percent of the cities' residents. Apartments, businesses, churches and the school are all in that one building. It even has a bed and breakfast for tourists to enjoy.

Since Nancy gets extremely seasick, she and Betsy intended to hike in the Chugach National Forest, the second largest in the United States, while Maurene and I would take a tour of Prince Edward Sound. Even though we were going two by land and two by sea, we would all be gifted with incredible views of the glaciated Chugach Mountains. We split paths, Nancy and Betsy headed for the mountains and Maurene and I joined the boat tour.

The captain said we would have an exceptional day for glacier viewing, that the glaciers would be at their "best blue." Maybe he always said that, but we were stunned by the enormous glaciers and their beauty. A picture can never convey being up close and personal with a living, breathing glacier. Those walls of ice were an incredible blue. Maurene and I stared in awe and the glaciers stared majestically right back.

As we cruised the Sound, we saw sea otters, seals, bald eagles, kitty-wakes, twenty-six of the one hundred fifty glaciers the Sound contains, and a tremendous calving at the Harriman Glacier. Maurene and I agreed that we could do this cruise every day while in Alaska and always be enthralled.

The train ride back to Portage, where we left our car, was just as delightful as the ride in. We even saw a bear in a tree right beside our window as we sped by.

On one of our stops along Cook's Inlet after leaving Portage, we were fortunate to see a pod of six Beluga Whales, also called "white whales" or "sea canaries." They are one of the most vocal of all whales because of the wide range of sounds they make. As we watched them, it seemed as though they were smiling at us. They were such gentle, beautiful creatures. What a gift to see them in the wild.

Unfortunately, I recently read that Cook's Inlet now has a population of approximately three hundred Beluga Whales and they are listed as critically endangered. Things like this make my heart cry. I believe that whatever we do to nature, we also do to ourselves.

As we journeyed closer to Anchorage, we stopped at a wildlife viewing area. With all the marsh in front of us, it looked like moose country. Walking onto the boardwalk, we thought we could see a moose way off in the distance. We used binoculars to make sure. All of us began a chant urging the moose to come closer which she did, so we continued "here moose" until she was about twenty feet from us.

We couldn't believe our good luck! She proceeded to run to the right, pose, and then run to the left and pose again picture perfect. She stayed right with us the hour we were there. Among the four of us, I know we took five hundred pictures of that beautiful moose. We all fell in love with her and when we left we thanked her for sharing this special time with us.

What a first day in Alaska we had. The scenic train ride, Whittier, Prince Edward Sound, the Chugach Mountains, Beluga Whales, and one very friendly moose. Wow!

The city of Anchorage and its surrounding area offers such a variety of things to do. We tried our best to sample as many of them as we could in our three days there.

On a semi-drizzling day, we took an interesting shuttle tour of the city and visited a very informative museum of Indian culture. The next day we drove south from Anchorage to hike Flattop Mountain and to see the bore tide at Turnagain Arm. Cook's Inlet has the second largest tide in the world with a thirty-five foot change. The wall of water can reach ten feet tall with speeds up to fifteen miles per hour. This bore tide is the only one in the world surrounded by mountains. It is easy to see as the highway runs along Cook's Inlet.

The day we were there the tide reached maybe three feet. It was impressive! The speed at which it advances was thrilling. It made my heart beat faster. Even though the speed of rushing water was only supposed to be fifteen miles an hour, I knew it was sixty!

Our third day in Anchorage, we drove north to the Eagle River Nature Center to hike Rendezvous Peak. Like Flattop Mountain, this one was so much fun to climb. Both mountains had panoramic views of Anchorage and Cook's Inlet. While hiking through the woods on Rendezvous Peak with Betsy leading, Nancy and then myself, we had our first bear encounter. Two huge, furry creatures bounded from the bushes onto the trail just ahead of us. Both Betsy and I jumped behind Nancy.

We soon realized in front of us were two gigantic black dogs. Nancy looked at the two of us cowering behind her and told us, "Now I know what I am, bear bait!" The dogs were very friendly, but Nancy still reminds us that we hid behind her in time of trouble. Betsy and I have no reasonable explanation for this. (We mistook Nancy for a tree?) She is tall. (We are cowards?)

Before we leave Anchorage, I must mention the flowers in the area. They were varied and beautiful, but the one that grabbed my attention was the dandelion. In Minnesota, my home state, the dandelion is basically thought to be a weed. I always loved that perky, yellow flower and cheered it on. Now, in Alaska, the dandelion is probably five times bigger and this "flower" is planted along paths and in flower beds. The dandelion had respect. I loved that!

Driving south our next destination was Seward and the Kenai Peninsula. The highway between Anchorage and Seward is designated a National Forest Scenic Byway. Every one of the one hundred twenty-seven miles was a wonder with forests, rivers, lakes, mountains and valleys alternating in view. The best part was that we would get to do it all over again on the way to Denali.

It was love at first sight with the quaint town of Seward surrounded by Resurrection Bay and the Kenai Mountains. Our goal was to climb to the top of the Harding Icefield in the Kenai Fjords National Park.

From the town of Seward it was only a short, scenic drive to the park. When we arrived at the ranger station, we discovered we would have the good karma of being guided up the ice field by one of the rangers. Ranger Rae was making her first inspection hike of the season. She was a little gal full of vim and vigor. She was also very generous, and brought homemade chocolate chip cookies to share.

From the nature center it was a short walk to the toe of

Exit Glacier. It is one of the thirty-five plus glaciers that flow off the Harding Icefield. Markers had been placed along the pathway to show the glacier's decline over the past one hundred twenty years. As we walked past the markers it became quite eerie as the recession greatly accelerated as we approached the glacier and the current date. We were seeing the effects of global warming as of 1995. It wasn't reassuring.

The Exit Glacier was enormous and beautifully blue. We walked along the Glacier Trail until we reached the ice field marker. Maurene left us there to explore more of the Exit Glacier Trail. Ranger Rae assured us she would be safe and that there was a lot to see at the park and at the ranger station. There were so many people on the Glacier Trail and Maurene never met a stranger, so we knew she wouldn't be lonely. I wanted her with me, but I knew this hike would be too steep for her.

Once on the Harding Icefield Trail, we walked through luscious green foliage and beside mountain streams. Many waterfalls greeted us as we meandered along. It didn't take much time for the trail to become vertical. It climbs one thousand feet per mile for four miles. About half way up we began trudging through snow. We were sinking to our boot tops with each step. It was strenuous, but the view of the mountains surrounding us and the snow path ahead was so incredibly beautiful that it peaked our spirits.

The excitement of where we were and what we were doing just propelled us up the mountain. Near the top, we stopped for another break, and Ranger Rae again shared her bottomless bag of cookies. As we enjoyed the view, Betsy expressed it all, "A mountain and a cookie, what could be better?"

At the top of the ice field, Ranger Rae took pictures with Nancy, Betsy, and me perched on an outcropping of rocks. She said we were now "Nunataks," a lonely peak. It is the term for mountain tops surrounded in ice.

So Nunataks we became at the top of the Harding Icefield, surrounded by seven hundred square miles of ice, snow, and snow capped mountains. It was the only time upon reaching the summit of a mountain that I felt I was truly on top of the world. It was glorious!

After a good night's rest, we wanted to explore Mt. Marathon. It was located in the Kenai Mountains surrounding Seward. A famous race was held there every Fourth of July from downtown Seward to the top of Mt. Marathon and back. The very first race resulted from a bar room bet by locals back in the early 1900's. The bet was to run to the top of Mt. Marathon (4,826 feet) three miles round trip in 60 minutes. The runner lost his bet with 62 minutes. The first official open race was in 1915.

Now it is the fastest, hardest, most dangerous, bloodiest and shortest race of its kind. There is a 3,022 foot elevation gain in about 1.5 miles. With an average slope of 34 degrees, up to 60 degrees in places, over rocks and scree, it is not for your casual runner/climber. This is the quintessential 5K race. There are usually as many as 800 participants. The record time is approximately 41 minutes for men, 48 for women, and juniors,

34 minutes. There can be a lot of injuries. Ambulances await the runners at the bottom.

For mere mortals this would be a day hike. This is the mountain Nancy and Betsy wanted to tackle. Nevertheless, we dropped the two off at the base of the mountain at the trail head. There isn't any long approach to this mountain. All 4,826 feet of it rises out of the land, almost without any warning.

That is only a slight exaggeration. The Kenai Mountains surround and dwarf the town of Seward, but Mt. Marathon seems to start right beside the road. After hearing all the statistics about Mt. Marathon, very steep, with lots of scree, Maurene and I opted to do a wildlife cruise on Resurrection Bay. We wanted to go home in one piece.

We thoroughly enjoyed seeing the city of Seward and surrounding mountains from out on the Bay. We were able to view seals, murres, and puffins. We were especially taken with the puffins with their little orange feet and matching orange beaks. It was such a beautiful day to be on the water enjoying incredible views of Alaska.

Meanwhile, back on Mt. Marathon, Nancy and Betsy were grabbing trees and fighting for a hold on the scree. With great difficulty, they made it about halfway up when they were passed by a father and his two children. The children were both under 11 years old. The man told Nancy and Betsy that it was best not to stop and rest because of the slippery scree. He passed by not letting his kids rest.

Of course, that was what the girls were doing, and he was

right, it was very difficult to rest and not slide down. They discussed the fact that if two children could do this, they could, too. Once again they started the climb. The slipperiness of the scree finally got to them and they decided to call it quits. Again, Nancy and Betsy tried to find a place to rest and while trying not to slide they heard rocks falling over to their right about 30 feet away. The father and his two children were running back down on a section that looked even steeper. His son sat down, and the father yelled to him, "Keep running, don't sit down or you will fall! Get up!"

At the time, the girls thought the father was very harsh and mean to his young kids. But, they didn't really know what the mountain required for safe scrambling. They did realize that what they were doing was not the right way. With a lot of slipping and sliding they made it safely to the bottom. Back on safe ground, Nancy and Betsy agreed that the man knew what he was doing, but humbly also knew that they could not run up and then back down that steep, slippery mountain. Not this day at any rate, maybe when they were younger!

After we all were finally back together again, we stopped by a river to watch salmon swim upstream. It was amazing to see them struggle over rocks and small waterfalls. There really wasn't enough water for all the fish. We then did some sightseeing in Seward, ate a late lunch and decided we wanted to do a hike by the midnight sun before we closed the day.

We checked for nearby trails and found one with a view. We headed out about 6:00 p.m. On the way to the trailhead, we passed a pie shop and Maurene asked us to stop. She wanted an "Alaskan Pie." I don't know why, but we teased her unmercifully about buying that whole, huge, expensive berry pie. At the time, it just seemed the fun thing to do, I guess.

We had so much fun hiking and knowing it should be dark that we lost track of time and got back to town after midnight. We couldn't find any restaurants open and we were hiker hungry! We had eaten all of our snacks on the trail.

When we got back to the motel, Nancy, Betsy, and I looked at Maurene holding her whole, huge, expensive berry pie. Wearing a payback grin, she said, "Well, I know what I am having to eat tonight." For supper Maurene had a super delicious slice of berry pie, but for the three of us, as we ate sheepishly, our slices tasted pretty much like "crow!"

Leaving Seward and heading north our excitement was now centered on the jewel of Alaska, Denali National Park, established in 1917. On our journey, we stopped at a scenic overlook, mile marker #135.

While we were there, the clouds lifted, and we were able to get our first sighting of Denali, "The Great One." Denali at 20,310 feet is magnificent. We stared in awe until clouds once again drifted across that mighty mountain.

Upon reaching our destination, our first impression was one of the enormousness of the park. It covers six million acres with only one road through it and one entrance. Private vehicles may drive the first fifteen miles to Savage River. Entry beyond that is only with park buses unless you are a backpacker. We are day hikers, so the bus it had to be if we wanted to see the interior of the park. We chose to go to the Eielson Visitor Center - an eight hour round trip ride. Even though we would rather have been hiking through it, the scenery was still breathtaking. We did have what is called a "Denali Slam," sighting the five big ones; grizzly bear, moose, wolves, Dall sheep and caribou.

At Eielson Visitor Center, we were able to get another glimpse of Denali and again we were so in awe that we all decided to take an airplane tour over the mountain the next day. When we got off the bus around 8:00 p.m. that evening, we were ready for a hike. We visited the tour shop, made plans for a Denali flight, ate supper, and then went to Triple Creek to hike in the midnight sun. It was a wonderful walk in the woods with beautiful wild flowers everywhere. The walk made for pleasant dreams that night.

First thing that next morning, we went to check on the Denali tour. The weather report was not favorable. We could keep checking back to see if the report changed, but we decided we wanted to spend the rest of our time in the park out and about with nature. We would stay optimistic about sighting Denali while on some of the trails.

So, our second day in Denali began by touring the park's sled dog kennel. The rangers were very informative explaining the care and training of these wonderful animals. We watched them harness the dogs and go for a short run. We all took pictures with the dogs for bragging rights. Rangers use the sled dogs in winter to patrol the park. How awesome that must be to experience the park in all the snow, and encompassing silence on a dogsled in the beauty of winter.

Now for a hike! We went to the Visitor Center for information to find the trailhead for Mt. Healy. This is a 4,700 foot mountain with an elevation gain of 1,700 feet in two and one half miles. This mountain would give us wonderful views of the area surrounding the park entrance. Because it was so steep, Maurene opted to do a ranger guided nature walk. Maurene had been doing most of the hikes. Although she and I may not get as far along the trails as Nancy and Betsy, we were still being up close and personal with the Alaskan wilderness.

Nancy, Betsy, and I began the Mt. Healy hike through the forest among green mountains. Colorful wild flowers greeted us along the path. Below was the Nenana Valley with the Nenana River winding through it. There were incredible views wherever my eyes wandered. Snow covered mountains surrounded the valley. The five mile hike took us three hours round trip and I wish we had lingered longer.

Our last day in Denali, we ate breakfast on the Denali Princess porch which gave us a view of the mountains. We did chores, some shopping for souvenirs and then went to Savage Creek to hike along the canyon river bed. The tundra and wildflowers delighted me, and as I had read, tundra was really like stepping on a sponge. We saw Dall sheep come to the creek edge to drink, some cute marmots, and a family of ptarmigan foraging for food. This was just a wonderful walk with nature. We appreciated it even more because it would be our last hike in Alaska.

That afternoon found us moving like sloths as we loaded our gear into the car. We didn't want this trip to end. Nancy went back for a last room check and to use the facility in private. Maurene, Betsy and I sat in the car chatting.

Fifteen minutes went by, then twenty. How much privacy time does Nancy need? We began to question among ourselves as to whether something might be wrong. We decided to give her five more minutes and then we would send a search party. Betsy was just getting out of the car when Nancy appeared. She immediately wanted to know why we hadn't come to look for her.

When she was leaving the bathroom the door handle came off in her hand. She couldn't get the door to budge and had been stuck in there the whole time. Nancy had shoved, pounded, and pushed to no avail. She called for us, but no friends came to her aid. We kept telling her, "Nancy, you always tell us you need privacy!"

She finally got the door open by putting the handle back in and somehow working it into place. She then stopped at the office, gave them the door handle, and joined us. Now that all was well, the teasing and laughter began.

It was cold and raining steadily as we left Denali to return to Anchorage. Maybe all the laughter from Nancy's dilemma and the persistent rain made our leaving not quite as difficult.

We flew out the next day again at the back of the plane over the engines. This time though, we were so thrilled by all we had done in the awesome state of Alaska and so tired from doing it that we were landing in Minnesota while still in the middle of our naps.

Since we had a three hour layover in Minnesota, my brother, sister-in-law, sister, their daughters, and some of my nephews joined us at the airport for lunch. The "Johannsen clan" had a mini reunion. This was a definite bonus at the end of our journey. It was just plain fun for Maurene and me to share our Alaskan adventures with them in person.

Two weeks after we returned from Alaska, I got a call from Maurene. She wasn't out of shape. It was much more serious than that. She had just been diagnosed with Parkinson's disease. She had known what she would probably be facing, but had wanted this trip to be as normal as possible.

On one of our evenings in Alaska she played a CD for us of a ballroom dancing competition in which she was a contestant. She and her partner were so very graceful. It was lovely to watch as Maurene was swirled around the dance floor in her flowing blue dress. We are so thankful she shared that with us.

Maurene courageously battled Parkinson's disease for the next twenty years. We did several family trips together and she was always our motivator. She was my hero. She truly was a "woman with spirit." In my heart she is still.

Chapter Five

California—1996

Yosemite National Park, California
Mt. Whitney, California

Betsy Campbell, AKA Cloudsplitter

B eing punctual has never been my strong suit. In fact, it has been a challenge that I have struggled with all my life. Fortunately, I have been blessed with understanding and patient friends, which is a good thing, otherwise I might not have any.

On July 23, 1996, my husband dropped me off at the Manchester, New Hampshire, airport 20 minutes before my plane's departure. This was, of course, not his fault. I tend to delay any appointment to the zenith moment. Unfortunately for me, the plane left 20 minutes early, and there I was standing in an empty waiting area. (I might add that this was not the first time I was greeted by an empty waiting area, but in my defense, that other time was not completely my fault- I like to think).

The next flight out to Fresno, California was in five hours. This was a pickle. Nancy and Cleo would be waiting for my plane in California, along with an old friend of Cleo's whom I had not yet met. (Talk about first impressions!)

Her name was Doris Graham and she was a fellow teacher. Cleo had met Doris when she went to Guam to teach at an air force base elementary school. It still amazes me to think that Cleo, from a little town in Minnesota, had the courage to fly alone to the tiny island of Guam for a teaching job, but she did and there she made and met lifelong friends and had incredible adventures with those friends. Cleo being Cleo, not only had those wonderful times, but also met her future husband while she was there. This gal really knows how to pack in the fun.

Doris was flying to Fresno from her home in Portland, Oregon. So how was I to let anyone know of my delay? This was all before cell phones and one had to rely on the wall of payphones. Still, there was no way to reach the girls even if a payphone was available. So, I did nothing.

By the time I landed in Fresno five hours late, I was tired, frustrated and basically in a bad mood and generally out of it. Not only that, but I got off the plane and didn't recognize anyone.

No one was there to greet me. I was getting more upset by the moment, but when the crowd dispersed, I noticed a short, dark haired lady holding a sign that said "Campbell." *Uh, oh, this is not good,* I thought, but having no other options, I walked over to her and said, "Hi, I'm Betsy Campbell."

In an almost bored, (or was it me projecting my bad mood on her), this somber little lady informed me that Cleo and Nancy's plane had been delayed and they were still in Florida. OMG, I thought, this was getting worse and worse. I just wanted a bed, a drink or home. I thought about getting back on the plane and letting it take me anywhere it was going, hopefully east.

I did manage to get out, "Gosh, that's awful," and I meant it. When seconds later Cleo and Nancy popped out from behind the near wall and said, "Surprise!" all peppy like. I tried my best to shake my funk and be excited to see them. Honestly, I was thrilled to see them as I had no idea what I was going to do otherwise.

The mysterious lady with the sign, which was a folded grocery bag, turned out to be Doris. Their little, cruel trick worked out great as I did not know what Doris looked like. They had used their waiting time wisely and got the rental car, maps and did some shopping. So, after I forgave them their cruelty, and they forgave me my errancy, we got in the car and drove to Yosemite Valley via Sequoia Grove. (I told you I had some fabulous friends).

We had booked a rustic cabin at the bottom of the valley with no air conditioning. There was a community bathroom not too far away that serviced all the cabins nearby and fortunately was for women only. It was very hot and stuffy in the cabin, so we left the windows open hoping the air would blow in through the screens. I had the single cot by the screen door which was welcoming and comfortable. Unfortunately, it was beside one of the main corridors to the bathroom and many times throughout the course of the night ladies with flash lights passed by on their way to and from the bathroom, my bunk mates included. They were very quiet, other than figuring out how to unlock the screen door and to the banging and slamming of the same. Still, it was a good night's sleep and it was chilly and refreshing by morning.

Our first hike was to the top of Yosemite Falls which was 7.6 miles round trip. Soon, Doris and I were talking and walking at a comfortable pace, and I got to know this extraordinary lady. She had traveled and hiked around the world with her husband. This included doing marathons and trekking in the Himalayan Mountains with porters, so I was duly impressed.

This dynamo had to be under five feet as she was even shorter than Cleo, but she was all muscle, no fat anywhere. She had a wonderful personality and was full of spitfire and was up for anything and everything. I felt I was in very good hands and would have followed her to the ends of the earth, and why not? She had already been there and back.

The views were just spectacular at the top of the falls, and it was easy to see why Ansel Adams had taken so many beautiful photographs of the area. There was a museum of his work down in the valley that we made a note to visit. Until then, we reveled in our own full color photographs which, of course, did not hold a candle to his or what we could see with our eyes. We waited for Nancy and Cleo at the top of the falls where we found a great spot to have our packed lunches. Smooth boulders lined the water's edge and gave us a comfortable and cool spot to eat and enjoy.

We were taking a quick snooze on the warm rocks when someone noticed we had a visitor just around a rock bend across the river. It was a young man totally naked testing the water with his foot. The surprising thing for us was not that he was naked, but that he was at half-mast. This news got us all awake and whispering to each other.

Soon, he walked back behind his rock only to reappear a few minutes later in the same condition. This went on for six or seven more times, with the man always retreating behind the rock. Well, he had our attention, but none of us could quite figure it out. We finally decided it might be some obscure form of a mating ritual. Unfortunately for him, he had no takers with us and we put our backpacks on and headed down scratching our heads.

Cleo and Doris told Nancy and me the story of their beginning. They met in Guam when Cleo accepted a teaching contract for two years after she graduated from college. Doris, born and raised in Guam, was teaching at the local high school. Cleo's new job was teaching second grade in the school right outside Anderson Air Force Base. Working at the base's school gave Cleo access not only to the base, but to the officer's club. Another bonus was access to beautiful Tarague Beach. These young teachers were pretty, single and making very good decisions.

Accommodations for Cleo and several other female teachers and nurses were individual rooms inside a round quonset hut. One wall of each room faced an open courtyard and was screened for ventilation. Nevertheless, the girls made it cozy and settled in. One of Cleo's roommates taught at the high school with Doris. It didn't take long for Doris and Cleo to meet and become steadfast friends.

They soon formed a group that included other newly graduated teachers from the Midwest. They called themselves the "Go Group of Guam" and spent their free time exploring the whole island. Summertime found them traveling to Japan, Hong Kong, Taiwan and the Philippines. These girls knew how to go!

Back in Yosemite Valley we took the shuttle to the Happy Isles Visitor Center only to find the area was closed. They had had an avalanche that caved in the surrounding area. Some of the falling rocks were 80,000 tons and created 200 mph winds shattering and smashing all the trees around the area. Acres were covered with a fine gray rock dust. Everything looked ghostly. It made me look around in case there were some loose rocks still above ready to come down.

We hiked up to the top of Vernal Falls and Nevada Falls trying not to think about avalanches. Both of these spots were gorgeous and had lovely resting places by the water's edge. While we were wading in the water several overly friendly chipmunks were rifling through our backpacks. One of these critters stole my nuts, crackers and Kudo bar, wrappers and all.

Nancy and I had started hiking all the high points in the United States and we had our sights set on California's Mount Whitney before the start of this trip. Whitney is the highest mountain in the lower 48 at 14,496 feet. The Mount Whitney Trail is 22 miles round trip and access is restricted in the summer.

We could only apply for a permit in May, which we did, and it was done on a lottery basis. We fortunately received a day permit, but not an overnight permit, which meant we had one chance to make it for this trip. Cleo and Doris were fine with the idea and now, knowing more about Doris, I was sure she was more than ready to do it.

We planned our vacation so we would end up in Lone Pine, the jumping off town to climbing Mount Whitney. We were trying to do several high elevation hikes first. We worked our way there via Tuolumne Meadows 8,619 feet. At Parsons Lodge they had carbonated water coming out of the ground which fascinated us. We thought it only came in bottles.

Next, we drove to Tioga Pass and hiked up to Gaylord Lake and then on to Mammoth Lakes Ski Area. This place lives up to its name with 142 ski lifts. We took a shuttle nine miles into the canyon getting off at Devils Post Piles National Monument and walked down to Rainbow Falls. We walked back up to Red's Meadow Resort through 600 acres of burned forest, then headed to Lone Pine at 3,000 foot elevation.

We wanted to get to bed early because we planned on getting up at 3:00 a.m. At 9:30 p.m., I called my husband. It was 12:30 a.m. his time and I woke him up. Oops! Got mixed up. We all tried to get some sleep, but I knew I wasn't sleepy, worrying and hoping that we would make it to the summit of Whitney.

Three o'clock arrived too soon, and we all drank as much water as we could manage. We wanted to avoid dehydration. Drinking it is the easiest way to carry water. There is something about water that just tastes awful that early in the morning, but drink we all did. Groggily, we packed our daypacks and another gallon of water each, into the car and drove up to Whitney Portal Campground at 8,360 feet.

By the time we got ready to go it was 4:45 a.m. and we lined up with our flashlights on, trying to see in the dark. Several people passed us going at a good clip. We were going to take our time and get as acclimated the best we could. Soon we had to pause for a pit stop which was a reoccurring problem the entire day especially with all the water we had inside us. The frequent stops did allow us to see and enjoy a spectacular sunrise as we slowly ascended.

When we arrived at Outpost Camp, the solar composting toilets were looking good, but once inside the bathroom, the great out of doors seemed the better alternative—not bad at all. Those toilets had a lot more composting to do.

At 11,000 feet, Nancy got a headache, was light headed and nauseous. None of us felt super. Doris and I felt the best, so Cleo stayed with Nancy and we continued on. We hated to leave them, but they said if they felt better, they would continue. We had to get going if we wanted to make it to the top. The scenery on the mountain was unbelievable, and we had left them in a gorgeous spot. The higher we went, the more spectacular it became, and we felt bad that they might be missing it.

When Doris and I reached Trail Camp at 12,000 feet, we were both feeling pressure in our heads, so we rested and had aspirin, water, cheese, and crackers. We had the 96 switchbacks still ahead of us to go up to Trail Crest at 13,200 feet. We weren't hungry, but knew the best thing to do was eat and drink, as much as we could. It did help a great deal to settle our stomachs, but there was little enjoyment as we had no appetite.

The switchbacks seemed never ending, and as some of the switchbacks were only several feet away from each other, it was almost impossible to have any privacy for nature calls. Plus, all trees and bushes had disappeared miles back. The only option was to be quick. No dillydallying allowed.

We ran into a man who was curled up on a rock moaning, definitely suffering from altitude sickness. We asked if he needed anything, but he wouldn't reply. He was in bad shape. Another couple came along and told him to start back down. He didn't want to get up, but they made him and started down with him.

Just before noon, we reached Trail Crest 13,645 feet. Doris was feeling queasy and I was very light headed. We rested for awhile, and I was looking over the edge wondering what it would be like to fall off. I was hoping I wasn't getting delirious, but was afraid to tell Doris what was going through my mind. I did not want to turn back, so I tried to concentrate really hard. I did make myself nervous enough that we discussed the idea. I also moved further away from the edge, which was difficult in that spot as there was edge all around me.

We had passed many guys on the way up that had turned back because of headaches or feeling sick, and thought we had done fine to get this far. Several people coming down from the summit advised us to turn around, and go down as it had started snowing at the top and a storm was coming. Just then we heard an avalanche off in the distance reverberating all around. We made the decision to head down.

We were gathering up our daypacks when a man came around the bend from the summit. We talked with him and he said it was his birthday and he just celebrated it the best way possible, by being on the summit and talking with God.

He added that the sky was clearing, and we had a perfect window of opportunity. Well, I looked up and sure enough there was a blue patch just overhead. The guy might have been suffering from altitude sickness himself, but it was the encouragement we needed. We continued.

It took us 3.5 hours to do the last 2.5 miles to the summit. It was extremely difficult for us to walk for any length of time without taking a rest to catch our breath, even on the more level sections. About one-eighth of a mile from the top, Doris said to go on without her. She wasn't doing the highpoints, and felt that this was close enough to the top to satisfy her.

I knew it was unwise to hike alone at higher elevations, but I figured I could keep her in view and proceeded to the summit. No one was there (wisely) as the summit was prone to electrical storms particularly in the afternoon. Years ago, a party was caught in an electrical storm on Whitney, and took refuge in the shelter at the top. The shelter was struck by lightning, and the occupants all died.

I wasn't thinking too clearly or moving too fast, but as quickly as I could, I made it to the top. I added my name to the log book, took a picture of myself beside the plaque on the boulder, and headed back to Doris. At first, I couldn't see her or the path and went into a sheer panic. I tried to calm myself, but it was definitely hard to think at that elevation.

I finally spotted her bright yellow rain jacket that she had just put on as it started to lightly snow. I was so relieved. When I reached her, she said she wanted to try the top. Back up we slowly went and took a few more pictures. At 3:45 p.m., we headed back down the 11 miles to the bottom.

No more than a half-mile down I got a pounding headache. It felt like my head was in a press. I asked Doris how she felt, and her head was killing her, too. We stopped for an aspirin break. That headache made going up the mountain feel good in comparison, and it never got much better until we were below 12,000 feet.

We knew we had taken too much time getting up, and as dusk was approaching, we tried to pick up our pace. Needless to say, our feet hurt, our legs ached, but our heads were beginning to feel good. We lost light at 8:45 p.m. and had to use our flashlights. Fortunately for us, there was a full moon. Once the moon was high enough to rise above the granite walls of the mountain, we shut off our flashlights and continued in the moonlight until we were near the bottom.

Nancy and Cleo were waiting for us with the car. They were quite relieved to see us as it was 9:45 p.m. It took us 11 hours to go up, 6 hours to come down. We had done Mount Whitney in one day.

It wasn't until we were in the car and driving back to Lone Pine that we found out that Nancy and Cleo had made it all the way to Trail Camp. Here they had asked everyone that was coming down if they had seen us. Several people remembered us, and someone told them that we had turned around at Trail Crest and were coming down. Nancy and Cleo decided to turn back themselves, so we would all be done around the same time. Once again, they had a long wait.

I went to sleep that night with a great big smile on my face.

The next morning, Doris and I bought our "Mt. Whitney in One Day" T shirts. The logo was of the profile of Mt. Whitney with a full moon which we thought was very appropriate, as we did have a full moon helping us on our descent. Cleo and Nancy bought "I Climbed Mt. Whitney" shirts. Although, on their shirts, right between the "I" and "Climbed" was a teeny tiny inserted line that read, "was right there watching while several people". We all wore our shirts with great pride.

It was on this trip that Doris came up with the idea of trail names for each of us. After much deliberation and joking, we decided on; Cloudsplitter (Betsy), Dustcatcher (Doris), Thunderfoot (Nancy) and Runningbehind (Cleo). The idea stuck and from that day forward those became our hiking names.

About 20 years later, I was standing in line at a grocery store in Florida, a tanned, muscular young man was standing in front of me wearing a Mt. Whitney T-shirt. I couldn't help myself and asked him if he had climbed Mt. Whitney. He turned around and said "yes" with very little interest. I replied that I had, too. He turned around once more and looked me up and down, assessing the graying hair, and asked, "How many years ago?" Hmmm, so much for being too full of yourself.

Chapter Six

Rocky Mountain National Park—1997

Mt. Elbert, Colorado
Panorama Point, Nebraska

Nancy Humphrey, AKA Thunderfoot

This was our first trip to the Denver Airport. Its aesthetics and displayed artwork were quite remarkable. The peaked fabric roof looked like the Native American teepees and the snow capped Rocky Mountains rolled into one. We didn't feel at all like we were in an airport, but it wasn't long before that changed as Cloudsplitter's flight was delayed. At that time, we didn't have cell phones so we had to go to the ticket counter to see her status. We were going to have a long wait.

Not wanting to waste any time, Dustcatcher, Runningbehind and I decided to use the time wisely and get all our hiking supplies. (Of course, this meant the same old raisins, nuts and granola bars.) I don't know what time Cloudsplitter finally came in, but we were ready and waiting to head over to our cabin at Anderson's Wonderview Cottages near Estes Park, Colorado. Our trip there took us through Big Thompson Canyon where I had been several times before as a child. It was just as awesome as I remembered!

Our main goal for hiking in Rocky Mountain National Park, beside its awesome beauty and grandeur, was to prepare us for the simple and necessary task of breathing at high altitude. Our intent this trip was to climb the high point of Colorado, Mt. Elbert. At 14,439 feet, it was going to be another altitude challenge for us living at just above sea level.

We knew that to adjust to altitude, we had to hike high and sleep low. Therefore, we spent several days hiking at over 10,000 feet and sleeping at our cabin (7,000 feet). The Albert Falls and Flattop Trail in Rocky Mountain National Park were great warm-up hikes for Mt. Elbert. After four days, we headed to Leadville, where we would be sleeping at 10,151 feet. Sleeping? Sure!!

Leadville is the highest city in the United States with a charm and decorum all its own. Silver was discovered there in 1879 which led to the Colorado silver boom. The wealth helped Leadville become a lovely city with brick buildings, saloons and theatres. Surrounding this beautiful setting were numerous mountains over 14,000 feet. Many of the wooden homes were painted bright multi-colors with decorative trim. We were told they do that to bring some color to the town during the long, snow covered winters.

In Leadville, we stayed at the Mountain Hideaway Bed and Breakfast. That week, there was an annual conference of the High Pointers Club which Cloudsplitter and I had joined. This club was opened to anyone who had interest in hiking all the state's high points. We were all in agreement on doing Colorado's Mt. Elbert, and attending the conference the following evening. Don, one of the other guests staying at Mountain Hideaway was also a fellow Highpointer.

We had many stories to share and information to swap about the different high points each had done. The owner of the bed and breakfast gave us this advice, "Get a bunch of Snickers candy bars for energy, then go out and enjoy the hike." We did just that!

Dustcatcher is hands down the most mischievous of us. You have to expect the unexpected when she is around. She is also the shortest, so she is high energy in a small package. Needless to say, her personality is infectious and before we knew it, we had a new hiking partner joining us for the next day's hike. Don was going to start out the hike with us and then we would split up depending on everyone's speed. We planned to meet for an early breakfast.

The hike up Mt. Elbert was a nine mile round trip hike.

That isn't a particularly long hike for us, but since I spend my time between Florida and Illinois, the altitude and the 4,700 foot elevation gain, made the hike a major challenge.

Speaking of a challenge, getting four women ready for a hike can be an arduous task. We packed our backpacks and laid everything out the night before, so we could jump into our hiking clothes right after breakfast. How much water to take was always the biggest question for me. Water, being heavy, made me not want to carry any more than I needed. But with the high altitude, I didn't want to take a chance on dehydration. I don't know how much water was in a Snickers bar, but I was hoping there was a lot.

We left right on schedule at 6:00 a.m. from the bed and breakfast. We arrived at the Halfmoon Campground about 6:30 a.m. The trail began, according to my altimeter, at 10,100 feet. Soon, Cloudsplitter, Dustcatcher and Don were pulling ahead. In the beginning, the Colorado Trail was smooth with very little incline, but once the Mt. Elbert Trail veers off, the slope turned sharply upward towards our goal—the summit.

We soon started shedding our coats. Runningbehind hid her sweatshirt behind a giant boulder that we thought we could recognize when we made our trip back down. For a couple of miles, we traveled through a conifer forest, and for most of that segment we couldn't see much but the area around us. Just before reaching the timberline, there was a large area of fallen trees. From here we could see what we thought was the top looming in front of us, but it wasn't. It was the first of two false summits.

We decided to hide some more of our gear, water and coats, trying to lighten our load for the higher altitude hiking. After that point, as we started climbing above 12,000 feet, every few hundred feet called for a short rest.

We saw a father and a son hiking. They were taking small steps in a slow even pace. We determined that they must know the best way to pace themselves for high altitude hiking. Thus began our slow even paced steps.

At about 13,000 feet, I began to feel like I couldn't breathe. I thought I might have to go back down. We stopped for about 15 minutes and had some snacks, aspirins and water. The oxygen deprived feeling luckily left, though the higher we climbed the more often we rested. Of course, Cloudsplitter and Dustcatcher had left us in their dust.

When I get close to the top, I don't know what happens, but I often say, "That's it, I'm not going anymore!" Cloudsplitter was on her way down and told me emphatically, "It is right there." Reluctantly I got up, along with Runningbehind, and finished the few hundred feet to the top.

When we arrived, it began to snow big, soft, beautiful flakes. It seemed that the large snowflakes just floated down over the whole Sawatch Mountain Range! It was so worth the pain to see such an incredible sight.

We signed in at the high point register, took pictures, then sat down to eat lunch at the very top of Colorado. Many of the people at the top were fellow Highpointers. Along with talking to the hikers and videoing, we didn't finish eating until around 1:00 p.m. With much reluctance, we started the trip back down Mt. Elbert. The hike down was almost as slow going as coming up. We had to be extra careful of our footing because the rocks were now wet from the snow.

Nevertheless, we were on such a "Rocky Mountain high," that getting back down to tree line went quite fast. However, once inside the trees, the trail seemed to go on and on. When we got to the intersection of the Colorado Trail and the Mt. Elbert Trail, we just couldn't remember for sure which way we came.

It was now about 4:30 p.m. almost everyone was off the mountain. We decided to head down the trail that I thought was the way we had come. It seemed like we walked forever, not knowing for sure if we were going in the right direction. I thought, *if I am going the wrong way, how am I ever going to have the energy to go clear back up to the fork in the trail?*

I sat down for about 15 minutes to wait for Runningbehind. I was getting worried, so I turned around and started back up the trail. About that time, along came a couple of hikers who told me that we were headed in the correct direction. They had seen Runningbehind and she would be catching up to me in just a couple of minutes.

I was so relieved that we were not lost. We walked on down the trail to where Runningbehind had left some of her clothes earlier that morning, collected them, and quite happily we made our way down to the trailhead.

Meanwhile, at the bottom, Cloudsplitter and Dustcatcher were getting quite distraught that we were not showing up. Fewer people were coming down and they were running out of folks to ask about us. The last hiker reported that we were fine, but still a ways up the mountain. They kept their vigil, though, and finally spotted us. They were greatly relieved—but not as much as we were!

Near Leadville, in the Eagle River Valley, is the site of a U.S. Army training facility called Camp Hale. It was constructed in 1942 for what became the Tenth Mountain Division. Both Cloudsplitter's father and uncle were in the 10th Mountain Ski Troop Division during WWII and were stationed at Camp Hale. Nearly 15,000 men were specially trained to become airborne ski troops between 1942-1945.

Civilian crew constructed 400 buildings in this valley in less than seven months. Along with the men, there were 5,000 mules and 200 K9 corps dogs in, at times, 15 feet of snow with the thermometer reading of -35 to -50 degrees. Standing next to the marker that overlooks the now deserted valley, I could tell it was a very meaningful and emotional moment for Cloudsplitter!

Since Runningbehind and Dustcatcher are such good sports, Cloudsplitter and I had our eyes on another high point that was nearby—Nebraska! The speed limit in Wyoming and Nebraska was 80 mph. That made it a fast 2.5 hour trip to Panorama Point.

Panorama Point was 5,424 feet above sea level. It looked more like a gentle rise in a pasture than the highest point in the state. It resembled a scene from an old movie. The waving golden grass met the sky in all directions. The prairie scene was only interrupted by barbed wire fences and creaking windmills. Regardless of the appearance of being flat, it was higher than the highest point of 30 other states.

When we arrived at the Nebraska high point, we could see a herd of cattle grazing on the prairie grasses off in the distance. Not knowing the safety of walking in the pasture with cattle, we crossed the cattle guard and drove the rutted road a mile to a windmill where we parked the car. It was a picture-perfect day on the Nebraska prairie. The wheat in the field running parallel to the road was glistening from the movement of the breeze. Over-head a hawk flew across the azure sky helping set the scene of another high point adventure.

Filling our day packs with water and snacks, we began our trek along the Colorado border to the high point. About three-eights of a mile east of the windmill, we came to the Tri-state Marker for Wyoming, Colorado and Nebraska. That, of course, required several pictures. Continuing our walk eastward up a small knoll, we could see the high point marker in the distance. We slithered under the barbed wire fence that marks the state line. Heading in a northeast direction, across a section of grassy pasture, we came to the resplendent high point of Nebraska.

The hike took around 45 minutes at a very relaxed pace. Located at the top was a sign, a desk and a stone marker surrounded by a pipe fence. After spending a week in the beauty of Colorado, we found that the high point of Nebraska had its own extraordinary ambiance. As far as the eye could see, was the beauty of the vast prairie, dotted only by sparsely scattered farm silos.

As with most high points, there are always pictures to be taken and food to be enjoyed. This high point was no different. We enjoyed our munchies under the white puffy clouds of the great Nebraska sky, then continued our journey back to our car. An approaching line of cattle was headed for the water tank located next to the windmill and our car. Not wanting to end up in the middle of the herd, we quickly got into the car, bound for the road. The two hour trip across the wide open Nebraska grassland was truly a delightful experience.

We had a little more time in Colorado before we needed to head back to Denver, so we went back into Rocky Mountain National Park. This time we were focusing on Long's Peak, 14,259 feet, a 14.5 mile round trip hike. We decided we would just do what was comfortable, as we had completed our goal of the high points of two states.

We took the Keyhole Route which led to the summit. The Keyhole, was a striking rock formation, supposedly resembling an upside down keyhole. Imagination was required for that, but it was huge and the gateway to the top. In six miles, we reached the Boulder field at the base of Long's north face. Crossing that leads to the Keyhole. Again, approaching 13,000 feet, my whole body was feeling the effects of the altitude. Runningbehind and I were definitely living up to her name.

Cloudsplitter and Dustcatcher were way ahead, but we could see them as the boulder field was expansive. They had been joined by a young German hiker who was going their pace and the three of them made it to the Keyhole. Beside the Keyhole is a round rock hut called St. Agnes Hut. I can imagine that it would come in handy during inclement weather and may have saved a few lives.

Our friends went through the Keyhole to the Ledges and determined it was the place to turn around. They joined us, sans the German fellow, as he decided to go a little further. Long's Peak was a strenuous mountain and past the Keyhole required near-technical scrambling.

Once we headed back down, my breathing got immediately better. Now I could feel my legs burning, but the panoramic views of the Rocky Mountains were beyond description. If you could use one word it would be majestic. I soon forgot about my legs. It never fails to surprise me how each mountain has its own uniqueness, and no matter how many hikes we do, they are all spectacular.

Chapter Seven

Boundary Peak, Nevada
Grand Canyon National Park, Arizona
—1999

Canyon de Chelly, Arizona
Humphrey's Peak, Arizona

Nancy Humphrey, AKA Thunderfoot

On this trip, Cloudsplitter and I decided to do some state high points before picking up Runningbehind at the Las Vegas airport. On most of our trips, we only like to take a carry-on bag—no chance of lost luggage and no time wasted waiting for luggage. We rented an SUV in Las Vegas just in case we needed a four wheel drive vehicle to get to the trail head of the high point of Nevada, Boundary Peak. It turned out to be a wonderful choice when we saw the rutted, unpaved Trail Canyon Road.

Since it was getting dark, we decided to park our rented Chevy Blazer a short distance from the highway. That left us a 14.6 mile drive on Trail Canyon Road to get to the trailhead. We didn't want to attempt that in the dark. The plan had been to camp at the trailhead, but as darkness came on in this desolate area, we thought that might not be a good idea.

That night we crawled into the back of the Blazer, put out our sleeping bags and attempted to fall asleep. Well, at least the back of the car was better than taking a chance of being bitten by a rattlesnake.

Who cares if we went from 64 feet to around 10,000 feet, the temperature was 35 degrees, and we were sleeping on the floor of a rental car. Hey, we were young!

Whenever I wear a different shoe than normal, in this case, hiking boots, I am very prone to leg cramps. In the middle of the night during my few minutes of sleep came a very strong Charley horse in the calf of my leg. The way I usually break the muscle spasm loose is to jump up and walk on it. Really, there was no way to do that in the back of a car.

I tried to open the back door. No way would it open. Later I found out the child lock had been set. Cloudsplitter tried to reach over the front seat and unlock the whole car. Don't know what she hit, but the car alarm went off, Wong, Wong, Wong! Thank goodness nobody else was out there camping. She finally said, "If we are going to make such a fuss, we might as well start hiking."

Just before dawn we headed up the rocky, rutted road to the trailhead. As the sun began to come up we could see a lot of snow on the mountains. We were not prepared for that, but decided to go for it anyway.

The hike was in the Boundary Wilderness area. The trail followed through a valley, next to a stream with the mountains in view in the distance. The path didn't remain clear for very long. It crossed back and forth over streams many times and often disappeared only to reappear several yards later.

Once the sun came up a little more, we could see a group of wild horses along the ridge. The horses paid us no attention whatsoever. I had my video camera, so I was able to take a few pictures of them. That was our second time seeing horses in the wild. We also saw them on the high point of Virginia, Mt. Rogers.

As the trail became steeper, the altitude started to have its effect on me. I decided to hide my video camera. Cameras were much bigger and heavier then. It was very scary for me to hide a $900 camera, because I absolutely had to find it on the way down.

The trail wasn't bad for awhile, but as we got closer to the top the trail became mostly scree. I would take a step and have to fight to keep from sliding back down. Eventually, we would scramble to rock or bush, cling and rest, then scramble again, not exactly fun. The grade was 50 to 60 percent in places. It was here, with Cloudsplitter clinging to a small boulder, we realized we were out of our league once again. We couldn't imagine how we were ever going to get down. Cloudsplitter was also worried that if something happened to me there was no way she could get me down the mountain. There was nobody around for at least 35 miles.

At those times, I was always glad that our families never knew exactly where we were and what we were doing. Although, we always signed in at the trailhead registers just in case we came up missing.

We kept right on trudging up the mountain all the time getting more tired, colder, and hungrier. Eventually, we got to a part of the trail that leveled out a little. It was much easier hiking over boulders than scree.

We got to a place where we could see the summit, so we took off our daypacks and climbed the rest of the way to the summit without them. Finally, we made it to the top of Boundary Peak, 13,146 feet.

As with most high points the view was amazing. We could see California's 300 foot higher snow covered Montgomery Peak only a mile away. We searched for the USGS and looked all over for it or the log-in box but found nothing. Cloudsplitter was getting really upset because we couldn't find the USGS.

However, I was getting upset because my lungs seemed to be filling up with water. Cloudsplitter was still looking around when she realized what I had said about my lungs, and when she heard my lungs gurgling she decided we should head out after taking only a couple of pictures. Cloudsplitter was grumbling the whole time about not having time to find the USGS marker.

When we got back down to our daypacks, I was feeling better and breathing better. Cloudsplitter decided to lead us down a different way which she thought was a little less steep. After a short time, we were back to another part of the trail with scree. I got tired of trying to keep from falling, so I got down on my derriere and started sliding down the mountain.

I don't know if Cloudsplitter did that or not, probably not, because she was more sure footed. Eventually, we got past the scree, down the saddle and into the valley. We had to walk back up the valley about a mile to retrieve my camera.

Heading back to the car, we were fortunate again to see the herd of wild horses on the side of the mountain grazing. By this time, it was starting to get dark. Our goal was to head back down to explore Death Valley National Park. There we would sleep in the Chevy Blazer again. There were no towns with motels any place close.

The closer we got to Death Valley the hotter the temperatures became. We knew there was no way we could sleep in the car with the temperature of 100 degrees. Cloudsplitter had the idea to turn around and start back up to higher elevations. I don't remember how far back up we went, but we were able to find a place to park and unlike the night before had a semi good night's sleep.

Early in the morning, we found ourselves in Death Valley National Park just in time for breakfast. We were extremely dirty and hungry when we sat down in the park restaurant. We ordered our breakfast then I headed to the restroom where I discovered that sliding on the scree on Boundary Peak had left me with no seat in my pants. How do you walk back to your table when you realize your underwear is showing? My neighbor, Helen Carlson once told me, "You are too full of yourself. Nobody is paying you any attention, they are thinking about themselves."

Of course, now we would say they aren't paying any attention because they are looking at their cell phones. As I walked back to my seat, I sure hoped Helen was right. Of course, I blamed Cloudsplitter for the whole thing since she didn't tell me the seat was out of my pants. Cloudsplitter said, "I didn't notice." So, I guess Mrs. Carlson was right. Nobody notices me. You might think that was a bad thing, but it was really freeing!!

After breakfast we went to explore Death Valley National Park. We had been to Mt. Whitney, California, the highest point in the continental United States so now we wanted to go to Badwater, elevation minus 282 feet, the lowest point in North America.

When I looked out over the Badwater Basin, I was sure I was looking out over a big lake. Actually, it was all salt flats. It made me understand what a mirage would have been to travelers in the old west looking for water.

After leaving Death Valley, we headed back to Las Vegas to pick up Runningbehind for our hiking trip down the Grand Canyon.

Hiking the Grand Canyon

When we begin a trip like this, we have to try and take a realistic look at our ability. Runningbehind and I tried to get our legs in shape for the 7.3 mile hike down and the 10 mile hike out of the canyon.

To prepare, we climbed up and down the three flights of stairs at the DeSoto County Court House three times a week. Still, we knew there was no way we would be able to carry a tent, cot, food, etc. for the overnight stay at the bottom of the canyon. Therefore, we paid to have our equipment shuttled by the supply mules. Cloudsplitter, a seasoned hiker from New Hampshire, was able to carry her own equipment in her backpack with no problem.

The trip into the canyon was usually done as a circle trip beginning by descending 4,800 feet down the South Kaibab Trail. The pictures seen of mules walking into the canyon are usually on the South Kaibab Trail.

It looks like they are walking on a narrow ledge, but actually it was about four or five feet across and not at all scary. The awesomeness of the canyon called us to explore each switchback that led to a new and indescribable view. The rock colors, the lighting and the entire vista changed with each turn of the descending trail.

One and a half miles down the trail at Cedar Ridge, we had our first chance to see the mules as they made their daily trip down to Phantom Ranch and Bright Angel Campground. We had to become one with the canyon wall, as they plodded past us in a steady pace like they were totally bored by the entire situation. *Like I can recognize a bored mule when I see one,* I thought. Actually, after teaching middle school for 35 years it reminded me of a line of middle school students on their way to lunch.

After leaving Cedar Ridge, we walked around a large butte that jutted out almost to the middle of the canyon. From the butte, we followed another series of narrow switchbacks down the canyon wall to the plateau that we had been seeing 1000 feet below.

Finally, from the dark sheer walls of the canyon we got our first glimpse of the Colorado River. It looked too tiny from this location to have formed such a majestic site as the Grand Canyon. From this spot it was about a two hour hike to the Kaibab suspension bridge which crosses the river. At the bridge, we could see why the Colorado River is given a "10" by rafters!

At the bottom of the canyon were the Bright Angel Campground and Phantom Ranch which consisted of a dining hall, store, and cabins. At the Phantom Ranch dining hall, we had a great supper of stew and salad for $22. The breakfast consisted of pancakes, bacon, eggs, peaches, and orange juice for $17 dollars. I am not money conscience, am I?

For the night, we camped in the Bright Angel Campground. Runningbehind was all zipped up in her tent. She wanted no snakes or scorpions in her sleeping bag. Cloudsplitter and I chose to sleep outside on cots. We hoped the cots would keep us far enough off the ground that no animals would crawl on us. Sometimes it was hard to believe how lucky we got on our trips.

The moon was nearly full and the temperature was around 75 degrees. It was incredible to watch the moonlight's reflection dance across the canyon walls as it moved through the night sky.

That was where the story changed for me. I became increasingly sick as the day went along, apparently from some type of food poisoning. That totally ruined my plans for the hike back out of the canyon. I became dehydrated and the ranger/EMT recommended I be airlifted by helicopter to the Grand Canyon Hospital. I couldn't believe what was happening as Cloudsplitter and Runningbehind packed up and left for their hike out of the canyon.

They had to leave in a hurry to get out before dark. I cried when they left, as I knew I would be missing out on another great adventure. Although a helicopter ride through the canyon was quite an adventure itself. I had to wear a flight suit, helmet included. It made me feel like an astronaut. It was an eight minute flight up to the hospital at a cost of $250.00 per minute.

I indeed had the flight of my life around the steep cliffs of the Grand Canyon. I spent the day at the hospital hooked to an IV. After a couple days of rest, I was able to go ahead and fulfill my dream part of the trip. That was a climb to the top of the highest point in Arizona, Humphrey Peak, 12,633 feet.

Canyon de Chelly

After leaving the Grand Canyon, we headed to Canyon de Chelly. The canyon was now home to the Navajo Indians, but once harbored the Anasazi Indians. Many ruins and mysteries of the Anasazi people were found there. We all loved the history of those ancient people, so we were much interested in exploring Canyon de Chelly.

Since I had to be airlifted out of the Grand Canyon, I was very apprehensive about this hike. There was only one public hiking trail down into the canyon, the White House Ruin Trail. That trail was about 2.7 miles with a 600 foot descent into the canyon. It ended at the White House Ruins which was the site of a two-level ancient dwelling.

One part of the dwelling was on the valley floor and the other 50 feet above in an alcove. The canyon was a labyrinth of sheer-walls absolutely breathtaking in beauty. The hike turned out to be very easy with the heat being the only difficult part. The Canyon was very hot and dry for me being from wet and humid Florida. All of us truly enjoyed the uniqueness of the canyon, and were amazed by the centuries old history of the people that inhabited Canyon de Chelly.

Our next hike was to the high point of New Mexico, Wheeler Peak, 13,167 feet. On our way, we stopped at Four Corners, where the states of Utah, Colorado, Arizona and New Mexico join. It was fun to be in the only place in the world where my big foot could be in four states. We could buy handmade jewelry, printed T-shirts and keepsakes or try Native American cuisine.

As a child, my dad always took us to state capitals. On the way to Wheeler Peak, we went through the capital of New Mexico—Santa Fe. The capital was known as the Roundhouse, the only round capital building in the country. It was built in the New Mexico Territorial style along with elements of the Pueblo adobe architecture. We all loved the uniqueness of the building and its architecture.

The next morning we began our climb up Wheeler Peak. The climb started out pretty easy, but when we got to the tree line the trail was covered in snow. We thought we would go ahead through the snow, but when it got to our waists we realized we were not prepared at all for this 7.9 mile hike. That was one time we had to turn around. It was also one time that Cloudsplitter had actually stayed with us, so we all turned around together. That was not to be the end of our adventure in Taos.

Taos, New Mexico

After a day of attempting to climb the high point of New Mexico, we decided to walk across the street from our motel to the shopping center to get supplies. Runningbehind needed to cash a traveler's check and Cloudsplitter wanted a few odds and ends.

Once at the grocery store, we all went our own way. Since I am not a shopper, I got the items I wanted and started walking back across the street to the motel. I was about half way across the parking lot when five or six police cars surrounded the grocery store. Some of the police SWAT team came along the right side of the front door and the others along the left side. All had their rifles and guns drawn.

I went into a panic with both Cloudsplitter and Runningbehind still inside the store. *What should I do?* I tried to think logically, which was always a stretch. I didn't want to leave them, but I didn't want to get in the middle of gunfire. I decided to move away from the store and get behind some cars.

When hiking, I am the person that everybody gets behind when they are scared by bear (squirrels and chipmunks). It seemed like a long time that I was crouched behind those cars. It probably wasn't that long, but it sure seemed it.

Finally, all the police came out of the store, got in their cars and left. *Now, what should I do?* I decided to go back in the store. I was very upset, but relieved when I saw Cloudsplitter standing at the magazine rack looking through a magazine. I was so scared that I called out to Cloudsplitter, "Are you alright?" Cloudsplitter was in complete bliss and missed the whole thing. She didn't even see the police.

Runningbehind, however, was at the service department at the side of the store. She was their only customer. She had gotten out a check and was in the process of filling it out when the young gal waiting on her let out a startled half scream. The cashier had such a terrified look on her face that Runningbehind swung around and to her surprise saw a policeman coming toward her with his gun drawn. Runningbehind stared in shock at him, he stared at her, and put his gun away. He told the officers behind him to do the same.

The manager came running towards her and shouted that someone had accidently pushed the "Robbery in Progress" button. That was a bit scary for Runningbehind being the only suspect in a heist. I was glad everybody was okay, but oh my goodness, I was sure traumatized by the ordeal.

Next day, we headed to Albuquerque, New Mexico, to drop Runningbehind at the airport as she was not going to climb Humphreys Peak with us.

Humphreys Peak, Arizona

Cloudsplitter and I arrived at the Arizona Snow Bowl in the early evening. The plan was to sleep at the trailhead under the full moon and clear night sky. We wanted to get an early start up Humphreys Peak, 12,633 feet, the highest point in Arizona. It sounded good, but when we arrived at the trailhead a number of people were there watching the sunset. We weren't expecting to find anyone as we usually never have company on our adventures. We went ahead and looked around for a good spot to set up our cots.

We had heard on the radio that the temperature was supposed to drop to the thirties. We had our low temperature sleeping bags. However, we began to wonder if we should go ahead with our plan.

As the people that were watching the sunset started to leave, we decided to walk up to the deck of the deserted Snow Bowl Ski Lodge. We thought it might be a place we could sleep out of the wind. It would also get us off the ground and away from any wild critters.

As we approached the lodge, the full moon was just coming up and we could see that one of the doors to the lodge was ajar. I thought, *gee, it would sure be warmer inside!* We went inside and a few lights were on. We checked the bathroom and the light in there was on also. That would work out nicely!

While inside we thought we better check upstairs in the main room to make sure we were indeed alone. The heat was on upstairs, yahoo! Plan 2 was starting to look awfully good. Cloudsplitter then went walking across the dining hall when all of a sudden an extremely loud alarm started clanging. We looked at each other and I asked, "What do you suppose that is?"

Cloudsplitter answered, "I think it is an alarm."

"For what?" I asked.

"Cloudsplitter replied, "I think it is for us." We both turned and made a beeline for the door. Wow, we did not want to be arrested!

Once outside, the alarm was shockingly loud and reverberated across the whole mountain area. We didn't hesitate to make our way back to the car. Now what do we do? We were sure we had tripped the alarm, but didn't know what to do about it. We thought there was a chance that we had been videotaped. As each car came up the road we turned toward the still colorful sundown as though we were just there enjoying the remains of the sunset.

We finally made a decision. We would tell the police we might be responsible. Surely, we didn't do anything malicious. We waited for the police to arrive. All the while, the alarm was shattering the peace of the moon lit sky.

After 20 minutes the alarm stopped and still no official looking person showed up. Camping out here was getting less attractive by the second. Another 10 minutes went by and we got in our car and headed back down the seven mile Snow Bowl Road to check if they had room at the Ski Lift Lodge. On our way down, we passed two white security trucks racing up the mountain. We had waited a half-hour, hadn't done anything wrong and rationalized our narrow escape the best we could.

We had had an excellent supper and listened to an outdoor band at the Ski Lift Lodge a few hours earlier. We liked the cute cabins then. Each had a Franklin fireplace type stove that was cranking out heat. That was definitely better than Plan 1 or 2.

Next morning we drove back to the Arizona Snow Bowl, avoiding the ski lodge. There was a sign at the trailhead that informed us that Humphrey's alpine zone contained *senecio franciscanus,* a federally protected plant that was found nowhere else in the world. That area also contained 39 other tundra species found only in Arizona.

We began our 4.5 mile hike to the summit at 6:45 a.m.

The first part of the trail crossed a large field that went under a chairlift. It was not running on that holiday weekend.

On the far side of the field we entered an old growth forest of spruce, fir, and aspen. Those trees were some of the biggest aspens we had ever seen. The trunks of some of the trees were over two feet in diameter. That section was quite dark and cool because of the foliage overhead. After 1.5 miles, it thinned out and the trees began to get smaller.

We walked over many snow patches that were frozen solid from the previous night's temperature. Once above the tree line, we thought we could see the summit. By the time we reached the three mile marker the wind was blowing extremely hard nonstop. The trail was rough, with loose lava rock, and in a few places a little hard to follow.

The trail followed along just below the ridge line which might have been done to protect hikers from the wind. However, that day the wind was howling from the west on the side of the ridge line trail and seemed to be racing up the grade of the mountain. It buffeted us around and at one point we thought we should get down on our hands and knees if it got much stronger.

We came to a false summit, but from there we could see the real summit. It still looked a long distance away and at that altitude it was hard to go any faster with the cold wind. Several young men passed us in shorts while we were bundled in parkas and headbands. I can't speak for them, but the wind was numbing Cloudsplitter's left side.

Once we reached the summit the wind was strangely not

blowing hard. There was just a gentle breeze. A few people were inside the rock shelter on the summit. One was sitting by himself and looked very sick. We asked him if he was okay. He told us he felt really bad. We suggested he drink and eat. He said he had plenty of both, but didn't want either. Soon a ranger came up and talked to the guy. He seemed to be doing a little better, but still refused to eat or drink.

With the fellow under the ranger's care we left the shelter, found a protected spot and busied ourselves with food and water. We registered our names in the peak log which was in an ammo box. We then relaxed in the warm sunshine, comfortable in our parkas.

The view from the top was wonderful on that almost cloudless day. Even though there was a haze on the horizon, we could see the rim of the Grand Canyon where we had been just a few days before.

The 4.5 mile hike had taken us four hours and fifteen minutes. After several pictures at the top, we decided to head down. We immediately ran into the same buffeting wind.

The ranger caught up with us on his descent. We asked him why it was so pleasant at the summit while it was blowing hard all around us. He said he didn't know, but that it was always like that. He also told us that he was patrolling the mountain because so many people climb on Memorial Day. He mentioned the man huddled in the shelter showed signs of dehydration and altitude sickness. Once he headed back down his symptoms would be relieved.

Shortly thereafter, we ran into the same man, who by the way was packing a gun. He did appear to be better, but was moving very slowly. We were very happy to pass him and get as far ahead as we could.

When we reached the bottom, it was sunny and warm. We shed our ridiculously warm clothes and drove by the ski lodge without so much as a glance.

Chapter Eight

Mount Rainier National Park, Washington
—2007

Mount St. Helens, Washington

Mt. Hood, Oregon

Cleo Simon, AKA Runningbehind

W e're Back!
We had not hiked together since 1999, so this trip would prove to be a great new beginning for more adventures together. Various "life" reasons kept us from the mountains

for seven years. 9-11, the illness and passing of Thunderfoot's mother, and my husband's surgeries kept us home.

Thunderfoot encouraged us to pick a mountain as 2007 seemed to find us all back on our feet once more. Dustcatcher invited us to explore her state. We all got excited when we realized three wonderful mountains, Mount Hood, Mount St. Helens, and Mount Rainier were all close to Portland.

Flying from Orlando, I arrived early morning in Portland due to a direct flight and the time change. Dustcatcher and her husband met me at the airport and we spent the day at their home. Thunderfoot and Cloudsplitter would arrive later that afternoon.

It was wonderful to see Dustcatcher and to share old memories of Guam. She gave me a tour of her home. It was decorated with items from Guam and the numerous places she visited around the world. It was fascinating to hear the many stories from her travels. Our conversation eventually returned to our time on Guam, where we first met, and settled on one special Sunday afternoon.

On that particular Sunday, four gals from the "Go Group of Guam," (a group of teachers that adventured together) decided to go around the island. There was only one paved road that circled the island in 1964. It went through many picturesque villages and by beautiful beaches and bays.

Shirley, Doris, Patty, and I jumped into our Contessa excited about the day before us. We hadn't gone too far when we noticed a young sailor walking along a lonely stretch of road. We stopped and asked him what he was doing so far from the base. He explained that he was sightseeing and had not been able to get any of the other guys on the ship to join him. The ship was leaving the next day, so he figured this was his only chance to see the island. We invited him to join us, made introductions all around, and proceeded to show him the sights of Guam. Doris gave him interesting information about each village or bay we passed. We stopped for lunch at Pirates Cove, a favorite restaurant, and half-way mark.

On the way back he told us that we had to take a tour of the ship with him, because the other sailors wouldn't believe his story if we didn't show ourselves. They had told him he would never find any girls. He secured permission from the Captain and we had a wonderful tour aboard that huge destroyer. Word soon got around the ship that "girls were on board." When we stood at the gangplank to say good-bye, the deck was lined with sailors.

We made our exit a good one. In turn we each gave him a kiss goodbye amid the whistles and cheers from his fellow sailors. First came Shirley, a stunning brunette from Nebraska. Next in line was Doris, a petite cutie from Guam, then Patty, a beauty from Hawaii, and myself, a blond Swede from Minnesota. We all wanted him to have bragging rights with the guys that night. I think it can be said that we made his day, but in return, we had so much fun doing it, that he made ours, too. I wondered if he had trouble getting takers the next time he went sightseeing, or if he thought being a loner might have its advantages?

Dustcatcher and I were feeling like happy, young souls after we finished reminiscing back in the year 1964, and remained so when we met Thunderfoot and Cloudsplitter at the airport that evening. We were happy to finally be together again after such a long adventure silence.

The next day we drove to Mount Rainier National Park. Mount Rainier was an active, but dormant volcano. At 14,410 feet it was the highest mountain in the Cascade Range. That majestic mountain had 36 square miles of snowfields and glaciers. Our first encounter was on the Nisqually Vista Trail, a 2.2 mile round trip hike with an elevation gain of 463 feet.

That short trail started as a walk through a very green and plush woods. Along the way, we encountered mountain and glacier views, waterfalls, and beautiful wild flowers. That hike gave us a preview of what was coming tomorrow.

Excitement was in the air as we began our ascent of Mount Rainier. We were taking the Skyline Trail, a unique and varied path. That trail was a 5.5 mile loop with a 1,700 foot elevation gain. Destination was Panorama Point at 7,000 feet.

I believe much that is beautiful in nature has all gathered on Mount Rainier. We hiked through lush forest on an earthen path. We scampered on rocky paths with stone carved stairs and stopped to watch a marmot family at play. We trekked through snowfields, strolled leisurely past spectacular waterfalls, and marched across boardwalks over streams. When I encountered the first enormous meadow of wild flowers, I had to sit down on the trail beside them and laugh with joy at the sight of all those colorful, delicate mountain blooms. I wanted to hold that moment in my soul forever.

Because we had the good fortune of a sunny day, we could often see the peak of Mount Rainier as we climbed. Upon reaching Panorama Point we were able to view Mount Hood, Mount Adams, and Mount St. Helens in the distance. The view on a clear day was reverent. We continued hiking a little further until we came to a snowfield stretching up to meet the sky.

That was the "jumping off" point where only those with technical training can continue to the peak of Mount Rainier. We stood for awhile and watched in silence as a group on the ice field headed to their first base camp. That incredible day on Mount Rainier is one of my all time hiking favorites.

Our next mountain to explore was Mount St. Helens, an active volcano about fifty miles from Portland. In 1980, its eruption was the most destructive in the history of the United States. It reduced the height of the summit by 1,300 feet. The magma from St. Helens destroyed vegetation and buildings over 230 miles away and deposited ash in fifteen surrounding states.

Knowing all this and being close enough to see smoke still rising from its crater gave me an eerie feeling. The area had a stark beauty with the crater a grayish, ashen color, contrasting with lots of green and new growth in the area surrounding St. Helens. Dead trees were everywhere.

We chose the Harmony Trail, a two mile round trip hike, to explore the area. There were great vistas of St. Helens all along that path. The trail had a steep descent and then nearer to Spirit

Lake it began to level off. Once at the lake we resumed climbing among the huge downed trees.

In the 1980 eruption, Spirit Lake received the full impact of the blast. The eruption tore thousands of trees from the surrounding area and tossed them into the lake. Those log jams covered about 40 percent of the lake's surface. So much volcanic material was dumped into the lake that its volume was also greatly decreased. We were amazed that the lake still existed. It was also incredible to see how much our Earth had restored itself in 27 years. It was an area that seemed to demand respect and reflection. Our hiking there was definitely more subdued.

The last mountain we climbed that year was Mount Hood. At 11,249 feet, it was Oregon's highest mountain, and the second most climbed glaciated peak in the world. We started our climb on a trail behind the Timberline Lodge.

The trail grade was easy until we reached the junction with the Pacific Crest Trail and the Timberline Trail. The climb became quite steep as we headed to the Silcox Hut at 7,000 feet. We had open vistas all the way with Mount Hood always in view.

The Silcox Hut was a small rustic mountain lodge built by the WPA in 1939. It was almost destroyed in the sixties due to disrepair, but was saved by a group of mountain enthusiasts and their friends. It reopened in 1993 and was popular with skiers and for weddings.

It wasn't open when we arrived, but we peeked through windows and it was easy to see why it was in such demand. The furniture was all hand carved wood, and it had a rustic elegance that emitted warmth and coziness.

Mount Hood continued to beckon us upward and the next climb was to the ski lift at 8,600 feet. That was a continuous uphill, single file path through a rocky landscape. The area had been suffering from a severe drought, and it seemed as though we were climbing vertical in a desert. When we reached the ski lift there still wasn't any snow.

Mount Hood was usually covered with snowfields above the 7,000 foot level. To be at 8,600 feet without snow was totally not the norm. The drought had completely changed the landscape.

My favorite mountains have a snowfield. To hike up to snow level gives me an on top of the world feeling that makes my heart soar. The view from snowfield altitude is always spectacular, usually seeing 360 degrees. I always have a heightened presence of God. With that Presence comes the wonderful feeling that for that moment, in that place, all was right with my world. I was sorry to miss seeing Mount Hood in all of its snowy splendor.

We had lunch with a view of surrounding mountains and then just tried to absorb this special time of being on world famous Mount Hood. Since there was basically no snow almost all the way to the peak, we debated continuing as far as we could to the snowfield. It really looked like no more than an hour's hike.

Usually it was a technical climb of about 2,600 feet. There really didn't seem to be much snow on the peak either which definitely showed the severity of the drought. We felt this was a unique opportunity to get close to the top.

We didn't want to end our climb, but we had an exciting evening planned and needed to be back before dark. We had made arrangements to stay two nights at the Timberline Lodge.

Staying at the Lodge was a really big deal for us. Cloudsplitter always finds our lodging and she is extremely frugal. She usually finds places between one hundred to two hundred dollars a night which we split four or five ways depending on how many have joined the adventure.

When Cloudsplitter presented to us the possibility of a stay at the Lodge, we were all in shock. One night in 2007 was $250 plus tax per room. That is about what we spend individually for a whole week. We had much discussion among us and finally decided that this was a once in a life time experience and we might not pass this way again. We went for it.

After our hike we made ourselves presentable, enjoyed a delicious meal, and then we proceeded to explore the lodge. It was built at 6,000 feet on the south side of Mount Hood in 1936 by the WPA. Ground level exterior walls used boulders from the surrounding area. Heavy timbers were used from the first to the fourth floor.

The lodge was filled with wonderful murals, paintings, and carvings provided by local artisans when it was built. It was on the National Register of Historic places and was a National Historic Landmark. I totally enjoyed our evening immersed in the culture and history of the thirties as we wandered throughout the building. The stay there was worth every penny.

The entertainment that evening was the "Misty River

Singers," an all female quartet with two of the group being mother and daughter. They each played an instrument and wrote their own songs. We loved their show and left with two new favorite songs, "A Prayer Like Any Other," and "Branching Out."

On our way back to Portland, Dustcatcher told us she had one more surprise for us. When we pulled into the parking lot at Multnomah Falls, we could immediately see why that was one of her favorite hikes. At 620 feet, it was Oregon's tallest waterfall.

Fed by underground springs, it flows year round. It has an upper and lower falls with a foot bridge built over the lower one. During the two mile hike we could see views of the Columbia River Gorge, and always the beautiful falls before us. It was so neat to stand on the bridge and be one with the waterfall. The hike was not long, but it was steep. It was the perfect short hike, and two million other visitors each year must feel the same.

We found ourselves traveling back to Dustcatcher's home elated and yet wistful, for it had been such an incredible week. We had momentum and wanted to just keep going to another intriguing mountain.

It was fun for Cloudsplitter and Thunderfoot to meet Dustcatcher's husband, to see her home, and to share stories. Many hugs were given all around, and we left for the airport hotel to be ready to catch our early morning flights.

All's well that ends well for we were returning to Florida with a "three mountain high," and we can return to those mountains anytime we look at pictures, day dream, or share memories.

Avalanche Lake, Montana 1993.

LEFT L-R: Betsy, Maurene, and Cleo, Boston in 1992.

ABOVE: L-R: Maurene, Nancy, Cleo, and Betsy at our teepee in Montana, 1993.

ABOVE L-R: Cleo, Nancy, and Betsy at Ogunquit, Maine in 1992.

LEFT: Maurene, Montana in 1993.

BELOW: Nancy, Mt. Katahdin, Maine in 1994.

TOP L-R: Nancy, Sue, Cleo, and Betsy in Maine, 1994.

BOTTOM: Betsy on Mt. Katahdin, Maine in 1994.

L-R: Cleo, Nancy, and Betsy, Harding Ice Field in Alaska, 1995.

TOP LEFT: Betsy on Mt. Whitney, Califormia in 1996.

TOP RIGHT L-R: Cleo and Nancy, Mt. Elbert, Colorado in 1997.

ABOVE: Doris on Mt. Elbert, Colorado in 1997.

TOP L-R: Nancy, Doris, Cleo, and Betsy, Colorado in 1997.

MIDDLE L-R: Doris, Cleo, and Nancy, Nebraska in 1997.

BOTTOM L-R: Cleo and Nancy, Grand Canyon, Arizona in 1999.

ABOVE L-R: Betsy, Cleo, and Nancy, Canyon de Chelly, Arizona in 1999.

BELOW L-R: Nancy and Betsy, Humphrey's Peak, Arizona in 1999.

LEFT: Cleo, Mt. Hood, Oregon in 2007.

BELOW L-R: Nancy, Betsy, Laurie, Cleo, Jasper, Alberta, Canada in 2008.

ABOVE: Betsy, Doris, Cleo, and Nancy, Mt. St. Helens, Oregon in 2007.

BELOW L-R: Betsy, Doris, Nancy, and Cleo, Mt. Rainier, Washington in 2007.

ABOVE L-R: Cleo and Laurie, Banff, Alberta, Canada in 2008.

RIGHT: Laurie, Banff, Alberta, Canada in 2008.

BELOW L-R: Betsy, Cleo, Catherine, Nancy and Doris, Olympic National Park, Washington in 2009.

ABOVE L-R: Betsy and Catherine, The Narrows, Zion National Park, Utah in 2011.

BELOW LEFT L-R: Betsy, Nancy, Cleo, and Laurie, Grand Canyon, Arizona in 2011.

BELOW RIGHT: Catherine, Olympic National Park, Washington in 2009.

ABOVE L-R: Laurie, Nancy, Cleo, Betsy and Catherine, Utah in 2011.
\
BELOW L-R: Catherine, Betsy, Nancy, and Cleo, Cascade National Park, Stehekin, Washington in 2012

ABOVE L-R: Betsy, Nancy, and Catherine, Stehekin, Washington in 2012.

RIGHT L-R: Nancy, Cleo, Catherine, and Betsy, Rainbow Falls, Stehekin, Washington in 2012.

BELOW L-R: Laurie, Cleo, Betsy, Nancy H., and Nancy F., Joe's Pond, Vermont in 2013.

ABOVE: Nancy F., Mt Mansfield, Vermont in 2013

BELOW L-R: Nancy F, Cleo, Nancy H., Laurie, and Betsy, Adirondacks, New York in 2013.

LEFT L-R: Nancy H., Betsy, Nancy F., Laurie, and Cleo, Shenandoah, Virginia in 2014.

BELOW L-R: Nancy H., Nancy F., Cleo, and Betsy, Twin Lake Village, New Hampshire in 2015.

ABOVE L-R: Laurie, Nancy F., Cleo, Nancy H., and Betsy, Mt. Kearsage, New Hampshire in 2015.

BELOW L-R: Nancy F., Cleo, Nancy H., Betsy and Laurie, Twin Lake Village, New Hampshire in 2015.

ABOVE L-R: Nancy F., Betsy, Laurie, Nancy H., and Cleo, Cape Breton National Park, Nova Scotia, Canada 2017.

BELOW L-R: Nancy H., Betsy, Nancy F., Cleo, and Laurie, Grand Teton National Park, Wyoming in 2016.

L-R: Laurie, Cleo, Nancy F., Betsy and Nancy H., Grand Tetons, Wyoming in 2016.

Chapter Nine

Banff and Jasper National Parks, Canada —2008

Laurie Chandley, AKA Blueridgebelle

My phone rang one spring night at home. It was my Aunt Cleo. I had not heard from her for some time. She had been talking to my mom learning about recent activities of her children and grandchildren. Mom had hiked with a group of women called the Happy Hikers before she had to quit due to her health. She had asked me to go on their trips in the past, but my career and workload always got in the way. Through discussion about what I was up to, Aunt Cleo learned that I had begun hiking at the North Carolina Arboretum and mountain biking at the Bent Creek area in Asheville. She asked if I would like to join her hiking group for their trip to Banff. I said, "Yes." There was stunned silence at her end of the phone line.

"Don't you need to check with your husband, Bruce, and get back to me?" she asked.

I immediately said, "No." I was not even sure where Banff was, but knew it was an opportunity to prove to both Bruce and myself that he would be fine if left alone. I had not been able to visit my family in almost a year.

Bruce had been through two major medical events related to his esophagus over the past two years. He had torn it twice due to a hereditary restriction. The second event also collapsed a lung. The doctors had warned us that there could be future issues. Within a month, he suffered three shortness of breath events, and he was hospitalized while they searched for the cause.

The solution was exercise to strengthen his muscular system and decrease the amount of oxygen his heart required. Through the last events he had become very dependent on me for almost everything. His confidence about being alone was low. I was worried about our codependence issues. That put a lot of stress on me, and I was worried about what it was doing to him emotionally. I needed an excuse to trial his ability to handle time alone.

Cleo told me that they did not have dates yet, but knew it would be mid-summer due to weather in Canada.

Oh, Banff was in Canada. Okay then, it must be up around Quebec, I thought. A long way from North Carolina, but a good trial to show Bruce he would be okay no matter where I was. We told each other we would be talking again by the end of May to get arrangements confirmed.

At my first opportunity, I told Bruce about the discussion and that I was going. He was not really happy about it. He must have researched Banff quickly, because he came right back to me upset. It turned out that Banff was on the west side of Canada.

Bruce had called me during each major medical event. My feeling was he could call 911. I would arrange to get home as quickly as possible. The first week of every event was spent in ICU, so he would be well taken care of until I got back. He did not think this was very funny. In the end, he got over it. The plan to go hiking stayed in place. By the end of May, plans were set for a July trip date. I had been asked to supply a trail name. My sister suggested "Blueridgebelle" and I chose it.

My dad had been having some trouble with digestion and maintaining his weight. He was in and out of the hospital while doctors worked to determine what was wrong. I asked my sister, Lynette, if she thought I should cancel the trip. She told me to go as there was really nothing I could do.

I needed to book airline tickets. So one night at work, I pulled up online prices. While booking the tickets, I got Cleo on the phone to confirm the dates one more time. The days I had were Tuesday through Sunday which seemed a little weird with only four actual whole days in Banff. After checking the dates twice with Cleo, I booked the tickets.

The week before I was to leave Dad went into the hospital. I talked with Lynette again about cancelling, but she said to go. I was flying out of Charlotte, and decided to go down a day early to visit Dad in the hospital. Monday afternoon I went directly to the hospital to see him.

My brother had also stopped by on his way home from work. Dad did not look well. I felt maybe I should not be going, but he told me to go. He had been to Banff when he was younger. Dad had wanted to take my Mom there, but it had never happened. He felt it was one of the most beautiful places he had ever seen.

The three of us talked for a couple of hours. Dad told us he was getting tired. As we began to leave Dad asked me to take my brother out for a really good steak. I did what he asked. Bob and I went out to dinner, caught up and reminisced. I spent the night with Lynette and her family. The flight left early Tuesday morning.

Lynette dropped me at the airport. I was off on my big adventure. The plane landed in Calgary with no issues. Soon Runningbehind, Thunderfoot, and Cloudsplitter arrived. I knew Thunderfoot from a trip Mom had taken to Maine. Bruce and I had met the hikers for dinner in Manchester, New Hampshire, when I was operating a manufacturing plant in Hudson. I was looking forward to getting to know Cloudsplitter.

Thunderfoot decided to add me to the rental car so we could split the driving. I traveled often with my work, so I had no issues driving in new places. Everybody liked that. As they grew comfortable with my driving I did more of it throughout the trip. The ride from Calgary was scenic. We drove by the Olympic's site in Calgary. It looked pretty deserted.

The scenery became more beautiful the closer we got to Banff. The town was modern but with a rustic facade. The view down the main street was a mountain peak that appeared to jut straight from the ground. Many call this area the Switzerland of our continent.

We had gained many hours in traveling west, so it was still early afternoon when we arrived. The Happy Hikers always go to the local visitor's center to talk to personnel about the hikes and wildlife in the area.

The Banff Visitor Centre was located beside the Bow River near a park. In this case, the wildlife concern was bear. Forest service rangers also told us about wolverines. Bear spray was not required, but they did recommend making lots of noise while hiking on isolated trails. We bought the bear spray anyway. They recommended breakfast at Coyotes and the Johnston Canyon Trail for a first outing that afternoon.

We jumped at the chance to do some hiking after sitting on the plane and riding in the car. Off we went to the recommended waterfalls hike at Johnston Canyon.

The Lower Falls Trail was clogged with tourists as it is a shorter and easier trail to the primary waterfall. Johnston

Canyon Upper Falls Trail was just less than three miles. There were about five beautiful falls for viewing along the path. I was glad I had no issues with heights. One of the fall's viewing platforms overlooked the gorge.

We took this hike at our leisure. We asked other hikers to take our picture on a large rock boulder. It was a great way to start our first day. As the hike was ending, a slight mist turned to a soft rain.

We decided to take a quick drive up to Lake Louise. The next day we would be hiking the Plain of Six Glaciers and the trailhead was at the Chateau at Lake Louise. The Chateau was breathtaking.

The entire building was made of chiseled stone. The atmosphere inside was elegant with a classic European flair. The view through the grand hallway to the dining area was of Lake Louise up through the glacial pass. On the other side of the building we could view the ski resort. We walked through the Chateau gift shop and saw many local Canadian artists' work. I still regret that I did not purchase a piece of ammolite jewelry as a souvenir. That was a stone only found in western Canada.

When we were done sightseeing we drove back toward Banff. As we entered town there was a great welcome sign, so we got a picture of the group with help from a family. People were so friendly!

We found a local grocery store and purchased lunch items. The hikers try to eat lunch each day on the trail at the top of a mountain or scenic overlook. Lunch items included nuts, trail mixes, peanut butter crackers and fruit. Sometimes leftovers from meals that would travel also were used.

I found over time that I needed to make sure I had included enough protein in my supply. Of course, plenty of water was packed.

It was dinner time so we chose The Rose and Crown. We were all very hungry at that point and had a good meal. We discussed some options for trails for the rest of the week. I was new to all of this so tried to just listen. That was hard for me because I have an opinion on everything. We did some review of hikes Thunderfoot had researched that left room for adjustment if weather dictated.

During this conversation, I realized the other hikers were not flying out on Sunday. Their flights were out of Calgary on Tuesday. Runningbehind and I both felt bad since I had checked the dates twice when booking.

I would have to figure out if I could get a one way rental car or shuttle bus to Calgary on Sunday. It wasn't worth upsetting Bruce with a change to my schedule. By the time we got back to the hostel, we were all ready to call home and hit the bunks.

This was my first time staying at a hostel, so my expectations were low. The hostel sat on a plateau above the town of Banff. I was surprised by the beautiful relatively new post and beam building. It had a rustic finish, but modern design with large glass panes surrounding a huge fireplace and open living room area.

Quad rooms with bunk beds were set up in blocks with

bathrooms and showers in the center. We would spend our first three nights in Banff. This was the time to get to know each other better. We all shared our stories in detail. It was fun talking like girlfriends in our bunk beds.

Early the next morning, we took the Roam bus into town for breakfast. Coyotes was excellent and became our breakfast spot while in Banff. I checked and found that there were no shuttles to the airport as early as I needed to be there Sunday. I found a car rental place and booked for a Saturday evening pickup. Back at the hostel we packed our lunches and headed to Lake Louise.

The hike on the Plain of Six Glaciers was about 14.5 miles round trip. That was the longest hike I had ever attempted. Normally, I did three to five miles. I was assured there would be rest stops along the way. We walked from the parking lot across the back of the Chateau. Lake Louise came right up to the Chateau's large back patio. There were large hanging baskets full of beautiful flowers from the gateways to the Chateau. The trail started off fairly flat, but we could see where we were headed. We were going straight up the mountain range.

I was asked to keep up with Cloudsplitter, so that Thunderfoot and Runningbehind could set a slower pace. We walked along the turquoise Lake Louise during the first part of the hike.

At the end of the lake we started climbing. The trail was packed with tourists that morning. As the trail rose, it narrowed so passing became impossible. I began to lag behind

Cloudsplitter around mile five. I found a stone area to sit beside the trail and catch my breath. While I rested, Thunderfoot and Runningbehind passed me. That was when I realized slow and steady wins the race. I thought they would tease me for being so wimpy later. I was meant to stop though. In the distance, a large chunk of glacier came off with a boom. The pieces shattered into a million shards of ice sparkling all the colors in the rainbow. It was a beautiful sight. I was later told it was very rare to see that happen. It made being last up the trail worthwhile.

I caught up with the hikers at the Tea House. It was located about two thirds of the way to the top. Good lunch aromas were calling. The employees told us they hiked up and down to work every day. They had a big helicopter supply drop at the start of the year. The employees backpacked perishables in each day.

After lunch, we continued our climb to the top. Toward the end, the trail narrows to a single path along a very narrow ridge line with glacial rock down both sides. We could see Lake Louise at the bottom of the mountain. We took pictures to show just how far we had come. Only Cloudsplitter made it all the way to the glacial waterfalls that fed the lake.

On the way down, we found a small creek beside the Tea House. Runningbehind and I soaked our tired feet in the freezing water to refresh them. Hiking back down was much easier as most of the tourists had gone. By the time we were done with the hike, I felt like I was basically walking on my ankle bones. My feet were numb. It had been a full day with so many wonderful memories.

The hike on Thursday required a big breakfast. We went back to Coyotes as they had something to satisfy everyone. We were on our way to hike C Level Cirque. This eight mile trail was a little south of Banff overlooking Lake Minnewanka.

We found the trailhead parking lot just off the main road. It was basically empty. We all looked at each other and then acknowledged this was not the tourist trail we had been on yesterday. The trail opened with a series of wild flower meadows. The sunlight struck the petals and elevated the colors.

From these open spaces, we began the mountain climb into a dark forest thick with vegetation. The path was fairly overgrown. We saw mine openings that had been used a long time ago. I could not imagine climbing down into those dark holes to work each day.

The elevation rose very quickly. At one point I was leading. I was sure I saw something cross the trail way ahead. We began talking among ourselves more as we tightened up along the trail. Bears were also on our minds, so being loud was not a bad thing. The mountain range began to be displayed through the pine trees. We came out of the dense forest and walked along the edge of the mountain.

The scenery was stunning. We kept climbing up and up. It was very peaceful walking with no other hikers around. We began to space out on the trail as we each set our pace with Cloudsplitter in the lead. All sorts of wild flowers were blooming on the trail edges. I stopped to take pictures of them hoping one day I would have time to identify them.

At the top of the climb, we came out of the woods. A long narrow ridge trail to the right led into a boulder field below the mountain peak, forming a cirque.

A cirque is a depression in the side of a mountain due to weather conditions and repeated avalanches. As time had eroded the mountain, wind and water had exposed the geographic lines in the open faced crevasse. Up the goat trail we continued into the boulder field and sat down for lunch. Sitting at the top of a mountain, I feel close to the clouds. It is a chance to appreciate everything in my life at that moment. That is why I hike.

The entire Banff valley appeared down the long V-shaped mountain range. Lake Minnewanka sat like a light blue sapphire in the base of the valley. I just stood there and soaked it all in. The mountains were stacked on both sides to form a glacial cove. Climbing the ridge trail to the field was like looking into the mountain peak.

After eating I found new wildflowers in the boulder area. We sat for at least an hour to absorb the accomplishment of getting to the top and to appreciate the views. Small squirrels sought our lunch scraps. They showed little fear of humans. When we were ready to depart we packed up everything, policed the area and headed down.

I love going down a mountain. That was the easy and fun part for me. My balance was good so I almost skipped. Down, down, down we went enjoying the scenery through the pines again. It was early afternoon when we got to the parking lot. On the ride back into Banff, we saw cascading waterfalls coming off the mountain we had just climbed.

We headed to the Banff Gondola. Cloudsplitter thought we had time to hike up Sulfur Mountain to the top. My feet were saying "No way." I was really hoping Thunderfoot and Runningbehind would feel the same. Cloudsplitter was over ruled and we got in line to buy tickets. The cars were very modern and we felt safe. It was some vertical ride up. As we rose the mountain ranges unfolded from every direction. The 360 degree views were spectacular. There was some snow on the peaks even in July.

From the landing point we walked on a wood bridge pathway around a gift shop and store. We followed the little wooden bridges over to the next peak to see the Climate Center. The center was a small museum with many weather instruments and displays of living quarters. It was incredible to think that people stayed here to collect data through the winter.

We walked around to enjoying all of the incredible sights. The view from Sulfur Mountain is often compared to the Alps. It made me understand just how small I was in the grand scheme of things.

Since we still had time, a visit to the Banff Springs Hotel was next. The landmark was one of the oldest in the area. It sat along the Bow River, and it looked like an old stone palace perched on a small rise. There was an amazing view of the river and gorge from the large lower back patio. Along the stone rails were large baskets of pink wave petunias. A band was playing for the early diners on an upper patio. Now that was the life.

We stopped for dinner at the Salt Lic, a beautiful log restaurant with an excellent reputation for good food. Runningbehind and I shared a gigantic steak dinner. I felt a celebration was in order, so I purchased a bottle of wine to share. Once back at the hostel we settled in and relaxed. I was beat. That hike was the second longest I had ever taken. My feet were telling me just how many miles I had walked in the past two days.

I had not called Bruce the night before, so I went into the living room area of the hostel for some quiet. He answered at the first ring. I proceeded to give him all the details of the past two days. Once I was done he was very quiet. I asked if he was alright.

My dad had died on Wednesday night. Tears ran down my face. I was in shock. I moved to the outside porch to have this discussion in private. He had been asked not to tell me, but he could not do it. He could not pretend with me for the next two days.

The funeral was planned for Sunday afternoon so that I could make it back to Charlotte to attend. Now I knew why the early booking for return was not just a mistake. The Spirit works in mysterious ways that we will never understand.

I was so glad I had taken the time to see my dad before I left. He had really wanted me to go to Banff. I could not have endured missing his service. I sobbed in my pain and grieved my loss. I then worked to gather myself together to go in and tell the girls. I got in the bunk, turned my face to the wall and cried myself to sleep that night.

Friday morning after breakfast we left the hostel and headed to Jasper via Highway 93, the Icefields Parkway. I promised myself I would not bring the trip down for everyone. I had two days to go before leaving for home. I pushed my grief down and moved forward. I volunteered to drive to keep my mind busy.

That trip was one of the most scenic in Canada. It meandered along the Bow River on the south end. I gasped at the sight of Castle Junction with large wildflower fields at the base. I pulled off the highway and took pictures right there. The highway meandered along the Bow River to the south, then moved north to the Columbia Ice Fields.

We drove most of the day with stops along the route for sightseeing. Late that night, we found the Jasper International Hostel where we had reservations. We tried to enter quietly and get to our room.

Turns out our room was every woman's room. It was dormitory style with bunk beds. The lights were out, so we ended up sounding like the bumbling three stooges to our sleeping roommates.

To add to the problem the bunk mattresses were about two inches thick and covered in crinkling plastic. There was no way to be quiet. We had trouble not cracking up at each other as we tried to settle down.

The roommates were not happy and told us so. None of us got much sleep that night. The next morning we found that the bathrooms and showers were also common areas. I guess they were as clean as possible under the circumstances. That was a big change from the Banff Hostel.

In the morning, we packed our things and headed into the small town of Jasper. We ate breakfast at a local diner, then walked down the street to the Jasper National Park Visitor's Center. There we learned that this area was big for hunting, fishing and camping.

There really was no day hike the rangers could identify for us. All was not lost though as the center had a taxidermy exhibit. I was now sure that the animal I had seen cross the path at C Level Cirque was a wolverine.

After some discussion outside we decided not to stay the scheduled second night in Jasper. We would head back into the Banff area for departure to Calgary. We got a nice hotel in Banff as a reward for our lack of sleep the night before. That would put me in position to pick up the rental car that evening and be off to Calgary for my flight on Sunday morning.

The highway was just as beautiful going south. The mountain views were completely different from that perspective. We stopped at the Athabasca Falls with views of Mount Edith Cavell in the background.

At a variety of scenic overlooks we observed wide sweeps of mountain ranges and the valleys far below. We saw a glimpse or two of Mount Assiniboine in the distance. Next we stopped at the Columbia Ice Fields. The museum was very interesting with a large topography map so we could understand just how massive this glacial field was. Other displays taught the geological history of the mountains and glaciers. It was incredible how the glaciers were changing.

That information was driven home as we drove to the edge of the Athabasca Glacier. There were dates posted as we started down the road. The first year was when the glacier field was discovered. The further we went the closer those signs became. It was shocking how fast the glacier was melting. Years later when global warming discussions heated up, I would think of driving that road. I had to agree that something was happening to cause the acceleration of glacial melt.

There was a heavy mist when we got out of the car at the glacier's edge. We already had on our heaviest coats. We put on our rain ponchos for the walk from the parking lot. It was wet and windy.

The edge of the glacier was very dirty, but then rose in a turquoise wave into the mountain edges and beyond. We could see why the lakes were this color. The museum had explained that minerals frozen in the glacier created the wide variety of blue colors.

Tour snow vehicles were on the glacier. Based on crevasse information from the museum, I did not think I would be comfortable doing that. I now wonder if the glacier section I saw would be there if I ever had a chance to go back.

In the early afternoon we stopped at the Mistaya Canyon for a hike. It was a short one for us, but a good stretch after a long drive. The canyon was very interesting with limestone composition. The colors in the limestone changed based on mineral content.

That was what the Grand Canyon might have looked like millions of years ago. We sat on the canyon edge and observed the swirling movement of water through the limestone chutes. We could sense the water carving the canyon deeper as we watched.

We found a hotel with a vacancy sign as we drove into Banff. It was a beautiful log design. It had nice beds, a pool and hot tub. We checked into two king rooms. Thunderfoot dropped me off to pick up the rental car for my drive to Calgary. We found dinner at a local restaurant we could walk to. We loved using the hot tub later that evening.

In the future, I sure hoped that I could do a trip again with this group of wonderful women. I was up with the chickens the next morning and made my flight.

My sister picked me up at the airport in Charlotte. She had a dress for me to wear. I went to her house to change and then on to the church with the family. My dad's service was beautiful. I was so grateful that I was there.

Part 2

Banff – Sunday and Monday

Cleo Simon, AKA Runningbehind

Sunday morning Blueridgebelle and I were quiet in our sadness as she prepared for her drive to the airport. Our thoughts were focused on family and her father's funeral at the end of the day. I wanted to be with her and Maurene, Womenwithspirit. I would visit at a later date as my sister asked me to do.

Blueridgebelle booking her flight from Tuesday to Sunday, instead of Tuesday to Tuesday like the rest of us, was fate at work. She did not need to make any changes in her ticket.

The three of us remaining were all feeling sorrowful that morning, but we decided to keep our plans to hike the Moraine Lake area. Solemnly, that was where we went.

Moraine Lake was located in the beautiful Valley of the Ten Peaks. It was a glacially fed lake and therefore was an intense turquoise blue. We loved walking the trails taking in the awesome views of the lake and surrounding mountain peaks.

We did count ten of them. All of the beauty around us lifted our spirits and gave us a resurgence of faith and hope.

During our hike, we always kept track of Blueridgebelle's travel progress. We noted the time she left Canada, changed planes, and landed in South Carolina. When it was time for my brother-in-law's funeral, we stopped for a while and sent our love by way of prayers for all of the family. Even though we were miles apart we felt spiritually connected.

Somewhere I had found a brochure about hiking in Sunshine Meadows. I told the gals we needed to do that our last day in Banff. Thunderfoot thought it sounded great, but Cloudsplitter was not sold. The catch was that we would ride a shuttle to the top of the mountain and then hike the meadows at 7,500 feet. Cloudsplitter wanted to hike to the top of the mountain and then hike the meadows. In her way of thinking to take a bus was a waste of a perfectly good mountain. Thunderfoot and I finally convinced her that it was a time issue as we had to be back in Calgary before dark. Reluctantly she agreed to take the shuttle.

We did have one short detour to make as Cloudsplitter wanted us to see the Banff Hoodoos. Hoodoos are tower-like rock formations created through the natural process of erosion. It was a short hike to reach them and we then took pictures of our very first hoodoo sighting.

When we arrived at the shuttle station, we were told the "nice new" van pictured in the brochure had broken down and that a replacement would arrive shortly. We heard it before we saw it, and we were shocked to see a huge, old school bus come up the narrow road and stop in front of us. That was our ride to the top. We debated the safety issue, but the driver assured us he had taken that bus up many times. The opportunity to do that was now, so we got on the bus.

The bus did not go peacefully to the top. There were lots of switchbacks, a shear drop off on one side, and it seemed such a narrow road for the huge vehicle. The bus noises were equally daunting with a constant chorus of grinding gears, creaking body, and screeching brakes. I looked at Cloudsplitter and Thunderfoot and their faces were taut. I remember thinking, *If I get these girls killed, they will never forgive me for talking them into this.*

Relieved to be at the top, the meadows opened before us. We had four hours before return bus time. Cloudsplitter was off leading us at a brisk pace. We wanted to see it all. The trail took us through alpine meadows brimming with wild flowers, and led us past three beautiful alpine lakes. Throughout the hike we had the splendor of the snow-capped Canadian Rockies surrounding us.

Since the meadows are on the Continental Divide, I took a picture of Cloudsplitter and Thunderfoot standing side by side. One was in the province of Alberta, and the other in British Columbia.

We did manage to do the whole meadow loop and make the return bus. Cloudsplitter had kept us moving. We white knuckled our way back down the mountain and once again, we were thankful to get off the bus, but what glorious hiking memories we had made.

At the car, I put my trusty walking stick in the trunk for the last time, maybe to be found by another "frugal" hiker. During hikes I need a walking stick for balance and support. My Walmart stick had been confiscated at the airport when I left Florida.

Upon arrival in Banff, I checked with a few outfitters and the cheapest stick I found was $69.00. On the way back to the hostel empty-handed, I noticed a Dollar Store and went in for a look. Success!! I found a turquoise blue, broom-handle "walking stick" on sale for $1.50. It worked perfectly on every hike.

That fall my oldest sister, her daughter, and I visited Womenwithspirit, as she had requested us to do. We remembered and reminisced during our wonderful week long visit.

Banff was one of the most spectacular wilderness areas I have ever been blessed to see. The sorrow during that trip caused by the death of a beloved husband, father, and brother-in-law has dimmed with the passing of time. Thankfully, the great beauty of Banff shines forth in our memories.

Chapter Ten

Olympic National Park, Washington
—2009

Cleo Simon, AKA Runningbehind

Our destination hike this year was Olympic National Park in the state of Washington. A new hiker, Catherine, would be joining us. She was Cloudsplitter's friend from New Hampshire, and was a former nun. Cloudsplitter had given her the trail name of Wisdomwalk. The rest of us made a mental note to be on our best behavior.

The morning after we arrived, Cloudsplitter, Thunderfoot, Dustcatcher, and I took the ferry from Seattle to Port Angeles. From there we drove to Wisdomwalk's home. We visited and made arrangements to connect the next day. The four of us ventured on, eager to do our first hike in the park.

Hurricane Ridge, at an elevation of 5,242 feet was named for its winds of hurricane strength. Thankfully on our day there, we only had a light breeze. The views were incredible with the snow capped Olympic Mountains always following us beside the ridge. Even though the area was in an extreme drought, the trail was filled with the sight of lupine, paintbrush and lilies. These mountain flowers were hardy to survive such a rain shortage. On Hurricane Hill, we had a 360 degree view of the Olympic Mountains, river valleys and the Strait of Juan De Fuca. This gave us an awesome chance to have "lunch with a view." It felt so good to be together again hiking on a mountain.

The next morning we were up early ready to enjoy a day with waterfalls. Our first, Marymere Falls, led us through an old growth forest. Ferns and layers of moss were all along the shaded trail. We crossed bridges over streams and enjoyed the peacefulness of being in a forest. The falls plunged ninety feet into a small pool. We ate lunch there mesmerized by watching the water "fall."

We continued down the trail to Lake Crescent, a beautiful glacially carved lake. Its depth is about six hundred feet, and its clearness and reflecting light gave it the color of blue. Sitting on the shore of the lake was the historic Lake Crescent Lodge noted for its homemade lavender ice cream, among many other things. Thunderfoot and I couldn't imagine lavender ice cream so we didn't order any. As the other girls sat there smacking their lips, we succumbed and ordered some.

Soon we were declaring how delicious it was. Ice cream is not my favorite, but homemade lavender ice cream at Lake Crescent Lodge was fantastic.

I made a mental note that from now on whenever I am offered a new opportunity large or small, I will take it. We were able to stop at the Sequim Lavender Farm for some great picture taking of lavender fields before continuing to our next waterfall.

The Sol Duc Falls Trail beckoned us and again we wandered in the shade of an old growth forest. We heard the falls before we saw it. Going over a cliff, the river split into three side by side cascades as it careened forty-eight feet into a narrow canyon. It was a favorite.

Our day ended in Forks where we would spend the night. Forks had always been known as the rainiest city in the United States. Lately though, it had become quite famous for being the setting for Stephanie Meyer's "Twilight" series. We took pictures in front of one of the main attractions for visitors, Forks High School. Almost every store in town had something pertaining to "Twilight." It was a fun detour.

After a night in vampire city, we drove to the coast for a day at Rialto Beach. From the parking lot, we took a rain forest walk down to the shore. Once we passed through the pine trees and stepped onto the sand, the sight before us was a silhouette painted in shades of black and white.

Enormous white weathered logs had washed upon the black sandy beach. In the distance, several islands appeared as dark rock formations. Add the fog coming in from a gray ocean, and it gave off an ambiance that was beautiful and intriguing. It was the perfect setting for the vampires of the "Twilight" story.

Probably the first half hour at Rialto, Cloudsplitter and I were almost giddy as we focused downward on the wonderful smooth stones covering the shore. As we walked the two miles along the beach towards the Hole in the Wall, we kept looking for the "keeper" stone. One would be discarded as the next perfect stone was found. Both Cloudsplitter and I still have the ones collected that day.

Once we were at the Hole in the Wall, a large hole cut through a rock formation, we hiked through it, the trail above it, and around it. That was a great picture taking spot. We climbed among the giant logs, and ate our lunch perched on one. We investigated tide pools and found colorful starfish and interesting green anemones. For all of us it was a perfect day with the ocean. When I got home and developed my pictures of Rialto Beach, they all looked like they had been taken with black and white film.

Olympic National Park, established in 1938, covered nearly one million acres in which three different ecosystems exist. It had glacier capped mountains, Pacific Coastline and a temperate rain forest. Hoh Rain Forest was one of only four temperate forests in the world. It receives twelve to fourteen feet of rain each year. Rain forests used to cover the Pacific Coast from

Alaska to California. The Hoh Rain Forest had been awarded the distinction of being a World Heritage Site and a Biosphere Reserve by UNESCO. Its unusual ecosystem had remained unchanged for thousands of years. We stopped at the visitor center for our introduction to the area.

Due to the extreme drought in the area, what should have been a trail through a lush canopy of old growth rain forest became a trail of withered, brown lichens, mosses, and ferns. The rest of the foliage was also in distress. It was a little like going to a concert where none of the violins showed up. We did catch glimpses of the flora in its glory beside the Hoh River that runs through the forest, and in other patches of lush green that caught moisture from little streams.

We spent most of the day hiking along the river, discovering interesting plants, and nurse logs which are downed trees that provide a place for seeds to grow, small animals to live, and insects to hide.

Even though we saw the rain forest in distress, it was an inspiring hike being among Sitka Spruce and Western Hemlock that reached over 300 feet high and up to seven feet in diameter. We had seen pictures at the visitor center, and knew once the drought ended, the Hoh Rain Forest would restore itself. We Happy Hikers finished the walk with a much increased appreciation of that rare ancient rain forest. Cloudsplitter took with her the only souvenir from the forest. She was stung by an ancient rain forest bee.

Last day, in search of our last hike, found us driving eight miles up a mountain on a narrow dirt road that had no guard rails. The mountain views were beautiful as long as I kept looking up and not down at the sheer drop-offs seen from my side of the car.

The Lillian Ridge Trail was at 6,400 feet and I was hoping it would be cooler at that altitude. Leaving hot, steamy Florida I had been looking forward to days of cool refreshing hikes. Upon arrival we found Washington kidnapped by a heat wave. That day was the hottest of them all. At 6,400 feet, we were above tree line and the temperature was ninety-five degrees or more. Needless to say we had the trail to ourselves.

The snow capped Olympic Mountains were always in view, so that was delightful. The trail itself was like walking through a desert on the top of a mountain. There were a few patches of snow and a scattering of daisies and lupine that added a bit of color. We managed to find a tree and that is where we had "lunch with a view."

I was having trouble keeping up with the gals, even more than usual, so they took turns hanging back with me. It was a tough hike, but only because of the heat. We were all glad to return to our air conditioned car. Here we parted with Wisdomwalk. She would return home and the rest of us would drive back to Seattle.

My sister, Womenwithspirit, had once lived in a complex that shared a back yard with apartments for nuns. The nuns would hang their clothes on lines placed in that yard. All the pantaloons were white, except for one bright red pair. My sister never solved the mystery of the owner. I believe Wisdomwalk could have been that nun. She was delightful.

Once back in Seattle we visited the Space Needle and I got a wonderful view of my favorite mountain, Mount Rainier. We enjoyed our bird's eye view of the city.

We had to make one more stop before returning to the hotel. Pike Place Market in downtown Seattle was an original farmer's market established in 1907. It was a place of business for many farmers, craftsmen and merchants. Pike Place has around ten million visitors annually. It is huge!

That was where Dustcatcher wanted to look for a T-shirt for her brother. A hiker on one of the trails told her the market was where he found his. The shirt said something like, "If you must smoke, smoke salmon." Dustcatcher wanted her brother to quit smoking.

The "march" began as single file we followed Dustcatcher store to store. Cloudsplitter was keeping up with her, but after half an hour, Thunderfoot and I were beginning to lag behind. Each store seemed to send us in the opposite direction for a place that might have the shirt. I began to complain, I was tired, hungry, and wanted to give up the search. I was ignored.

On we went to the eighth store. That time Thunderfoot took up my "chorus." It was getting late and she was worried about driving in Seattle after dark, especially since Cloudsplitter was not exactly sure of the hotel's location. Thunderfoot and I both said, "One more!" On we went to the ninth store. One hour and fifteen minutes of searching and Dustcatcher succeeded. She got her T-shirt and we got to relax, and EAT!

Finally, we were headed to our hotel. Thunderfoot asked Cloudsplitter, who always gets our hotels, for the hotel's address. Cloudsplitter said, "I don't have the address, but we should see it on the way since it is close to the airport."

At this statement Thunderfoot was flabbergasted, and wanted to know just how Cloudsplitter planned on finding the hotel. Thunderfoot stated, "This isn't Punta Gorda, Seattle is a big city." Thunderfoot came up with the idea to drive back to the rental car return and have them take us to our hotel.

It was great to shower and relax for the evening, until we got a call from the car rental. Thunderfoot had forgotten to turn in the rental car key which if it wasn't returned would cost $250. Thunderfoot panicked, but found she had carefully put the key in her pouch just as she had done all week. Wow, we quickly hopped back on the rental car shuttle and returned that expensive key.

After writing this chapter in 2019, ten years after our trip, I did some research on the Hoh Rain Forest. What I found was not good. In 2015, the area was struck by another drought with some areas getting twelve inches of rain instead of the usual twelve feet. 2019 found Forks rationing water, dry foliage ripe for wild fires, and the Hoh River extremely low. That wonderful rain forest may become another global warming victim.

Olympic National Park was a truly unique hiking trip which gave us the opportunity to experience the mountains, a rain forest, and the coastline all nestled in one beautiful area. It has also taken a special place in our hearts for it became our last adventure with Dustcatcher.

Chapter Eleven

Bryce Canyon and Zion National Parks, Utah—2011

Kodachrome State Park, Utah
The Valley of Fire State Park, Nevada

Laurie Chandley, AKA Blueridgebelle

I hated to miss the previous year's hiking trip. For six months after my dad's death my mom was able to live independently. Then due to major back issues, she had emergency surgery that fused her lower spine. She never went home again. Her furnishings had to be packed that summer and the house sold by my sister and me. Mom was settled into an assisted living center. Every year she looked forward to watching the video that Thunderfoot took of each trip. We got to enjoy the trips together as we watched and discussed the videos.

The trip that year was to Utah to see Zion and Bryce Canyon National Parks. I educated myself on this area of the country as I knew nothing about it.

Utah had an interesting ecosystem. At one time it was an ancient lake bed. Later, mountains were lifted up as tectonic plates shifted. As the ground lifted and the lake disappeared, the sandstone/limestone bottom was exposed. The unique formations seen in Bryce Canyon are the direct result of wind and water erosion of that limestone and mineral lake bed.

We flew into Las Vegas to begin our trip. I had been to Las Vegas in the late 1980's and quite a bit had changed since then. Everything was much bigger and better including the airport, hotels, casinos and main strip.

My flight arrived first. I waited for Thunderfoot and Cloudsplitter in the baggage claim area. Runningbehind was the last one in. After hugs all around, we picked up the rental car with Thunderfoot and I designated as drivers. The drive to Utah took us through a flat almost desert looking country side.

We stopped at Walmart to pick up supplies. That stop was notable as it was the first time I had seen Mormon women and children in conservative dress. Of course, we were in shorts, hiking boots, and backpacks since it made it easier not to pack those items. I think we looked each other over with equal fascination.

It was almost a six hour drive to our cabin located between the two parks. We drove through Zion on the way to our residence. It was an amazing drive that began in the small town of Springdale just outside the park. There were restaurants, shops, and hotels. We stopped in the town to pick up some maps of the area.

I had taken over driving at the Walmart as we moved into the mountains. I was used to driving winding mountain roads in Western North Carolina so was more comfortable with that type of terrain.

The drive through Zion National Park had dramatic vistas on a road of sharp twists and turns. I enjoyed listening to the "oohs" and "aahs" of my passengers.

In some cases, I went too fast for these flatlanders from Florida. There were gasps and squeals if I got too close to the car ahead. I was totally focused on the curving road as it changed elevations. We came to a fairly straight tunnel with cutouts of vistas and this allowed me some moments to also enjoy the views. The sun began to set as we left the park.

We stayed at "Happy Ours" the entire trip which was a first for this hiking group. The cabin was owned by a wonderful couple, Dave and Karren. It had originally been her father's small hunting cabin. When the couple retired on the property, they built another home and expanded the cabin to make it a rental condominium. It was so sweet and rustic. The original portion of the hunting cabin had been made into a bedroom with four queen size bunk-beds. A central ladder took me up to the top bunk. It was like an all night slumber party for Thunderfoot, Runningbehind, and me.

Cloudsplitter took a loft room that had been added to the cabin. She would share it with her friend, Wisdomwalk, who joined us for part of the trip. A kitchen, living room, and two bathrooms had also been added. There was also a washer and dryer. This was high style living! We really loved being in one place and made it our own.

The evening gave us time to view the maps for trails and check weather for the week. That was important in order to plan the day we could hike the Narrows at Zion. It would be river bed hiking and there could be no rain forecasted. It was too dangerous to hike if there was any chance of rain north of the park or nearby.

Hiking the Narrows was something we all agreed we wanted to try. Our focus was to begin hiking in Zion and then move to Bryce Canyon National Park later in the week. Once that was settled we bunked down for the night.

In the morning, we had breakfast and headed to Zion. Our first stop was to hike the Canyon Overlook Trail. That hike led us to the canyon view we had seen in many famous pictures. It took our breath away. En route to the overview, we passed under boulders the size of large buildings. It was a little unnerving to be walking under them. In some areas I felt like a mountain goat navigating the small trail edging along the cliff face. What a start to our stay!

Our next stop was at the visitor's center for more park

information and to talk to the park rangers. We watched a video about the park and ended at the Zion Human History Museum across the road.

The museum explained the topography and formation of the mountain range. There was also information on the animals seen in the park, the history of Native Americans and the Mormons who named the park when they discovered it. That took most of the afternoon.

The next day we took the park shuttle bus to the area of the park where cars were prohibited. This allowed us to see that area of the park and stop along the way to hike a variety of trails.

We started at the Riverside Trail. It meandered along the river and into a slot canyon. Large boulders in the low running river called my name and created stepping stones for picture taking. While watching the video with my mom, I realized just how nervous that made Cloudsplitter. She kept inching closer to me with a worried look on her face without actually going too close to the river. We did not yet know each other well enough for Cloudsplitter to realize I had no real fear of heights and had excellent balance.

Next was the Weeping Rock Trail, a good place to eat our lunch. The trail wandered along the canyon wall to an area of widespread seeping water. The water sprinkled off the canyon face from springs onto lush plants that clung to catch the resulting spray. We sat under the mist and it felt good in the 90 degree heat. Erosion had created a viewing platform in the canyon under the boulder. From this point we could catch a glimpse of Angels Landing, another great trail.

The afternoon was spent on the Emerald Pools Trail where we saw the sun start to go down. Reflections of the mountains could be seen in the broadest part of the North Fork River. The trail rose to climb along the ridge line giving us a chance to see the distant cliffs. The sun shone directly on them and set them afire.

Zion was such a dry and desolate place. The plants and trees twist and turn to catch water and light. The mountain tops are white limestone that transition downward to graphic layers of color. Incredible mountain colors in every hue of red run from brilliant to dark rust at the mountain base.

The shuttle bus took us back to the visitor center. We had dinner sitting outside in Springdale as the sun set. The cliff walls were lit on fire and then faded into shadow. On the drive back to the cabin we made a quick stop at the Checkerboard Mesa. The mountain wall erosion creates horizontal and vertical water run-off lines in the stone. Once back on the road the others got a glimpse of mule deer on the cliffs just as darkness became night.

The next day was perfect for hiking the Narrows. We headed to a shop in Springdale that was recommended for advice on safety. They also rented special shoes that would keep our feet warm and dry. The others rented shoes, but I had an additional pair of good hiking boots. I hoped I wouldn't regret that decision later. I did rent a sturdy hiking stick. We headed to the shuttle bus for a ride to the trailhead.

We quickly reached the Narrow's entrance. The beginning of the hike forced us right into chest high freezing water. Well, chest high for most people. Runningbehind is short and was having trouble with the water depth, so she hitched a ride on Thunderfoot's back. After we got through this deep water, we changed our wet clothes and began to hike along the edge of the river beside the canyon walls. The canyon walls go straight up with only a small opening directly above to the sky. We hiked into and out of the river as the trail moved from side to side.

All of a sudden my feet slipped on the rocks at one crossing and down I went. I threw my hand in the air holding my camera high trying to save it, but sank below the water at the last minute. I came up laughing, but everyone else was horrified. I was glad everyone had pictures of the trip and I finally got them laughing with me. Mine would never leave that ruined camera. We stopped for lunch just as the sun came over head. It felt wonderful, so we relaxed and let it dry us.

We did not want that adventure to end, but the sun was setting so we headed back out of the canyon. On the way, we got to see a couple rappel down the canyon walls on one side and then climb back out with help from their friends above. We got soaked again coming through the deep part of the river, so it was a good decision to turn back when we did. That was one of the most amazing hikes I have ever done and will never forget it.

Bryce Canyon National Park was next. We drove all the way up the winding road to the top overlook. While similar to the color and geology of Zion the rock formations are completely different. Water erosion creates stand alone formations that are called hoodoos. They begin as thin walls, transition into arches and then as the arch fails the two sides become spires.

The views went on for as far as the eye could see with a low canyon range in the darkened valley below. As we drove down the mountains there were overlooks along the way to stop and see unique features in various bowls and valleys.

We viewed the range from generally decreasing elevations. Each stop was different. At 8,700 feet was Rainbow Point. It offered a complete landscape view of the hoodoo walls and intermingled pinnacle spires. At Agua Canyon, the land laid like a sand painting with hoodoos so sculpted that human shapes seemed to stand out individually. (I knew that was Bart Simpson at the forefront.)

From Natural Bridge there was an arched picture frame of the forest floor in the valley below. The rich white and red sandstone created every hue imaginable. The green valley ranges in the distance stood in stark contrast to the brilliant mountain colors. At Bryce Point the pure white limestone looked like scattered snow on the surrounding mountain tops.

Below were ivory caves in the wall face. I wondered how climbers could resist and then remembered we had been warned that it was dangerous just to stand too close to the edge as the sandstone was slippery. Observing other areas of the canyon can be like watching clouds. As we made slight shifts in stance, amazing statues appeared and we saw changing impressions of the hoodoos.

We did one short hike that afternoon. The Bryce Garden Trail was a short journey into the canyon. Dramatic views of hoodoos and the canyon topography led to small tunnels on the trail. I could observe how plants and trees clung desperately to the rocks. Plants have to be persistent to survive, although we saw a 1,600 year old Bristle Cone Pine. These hikes took up most of the day.

Thunderfoot does not like to do hikes with more than a 1,500 foot elevation change. Any more was hard on the feet and knees. The Queen's Garden Trail was a larger elevation change than that, but it sounded like a wonderful chance to see the base of the canyons as well as the mountain tops.

We all begged her to do that hike the next day and she finally relented. We promised to go at a slower pace taking lots of breaks. That would give us a chance to observe the hoodoos from another perspective. They are very impressive when looking up at them. The sun would hit the white tops of the hoodoos making them stand out against the red sandstone or blue sky. That trail wound gradually down into the canyon.

Everything looked different on the Queen's Garden Trail at the base of Sunrise Point. Lush grasslands and pines shaded the trail and cut the heat of the sun. Small plants and grasses brought bright greens into play as relief to the desert reds. On a section identified as the Navaho Loop in the base of the canyon, the ground looked like it had been painted in hues of cream to rose. Areas of healthy vegetation and trees other than pine appeared. A sign warned that a low area would flash flood in rains. We could see where a large log jam had been created. Since it was overcast and occasionally sprinkling we crossed quickly.

The trail led into slot canyons where the walls rose multistories high. The walls felt like they were pressing in on us. The end of the canyons brought us to a shear wall where the trail literally wove back and forth across the face. That created a switchback ladder to the top of the mountain. Once we reached the top, we popped out to see long range mountains, valley views, and the tops of the hoodoos. Thunderfoot was glad she had joined us and we all agreed that this was a hike like no other.

In the afternoon, we drove to a local state park. Kodachrome State Park was a unique find. I think that initially we were the only ones there. The loop trail began at a very flat elevation and wound upward toward a large stone arch. At Shakespeare Arch, Thunderfoot spied a bird building a nest in a tree. In this dry desert environment seeing animals was rare.

Halfway around the loop the view opened to broad range with white mountains in the far distance. Runningbehind and I paused in awe taking in the unexpected open grassland's view. Runningbehind whispered, "Can you see the buffalo?"

I said "Yes...yes I can!"

We hated to keep moving, but were falling behind the others. We wound our way back into the desert environment and to the car. The drive back towards our cabin took us through the grassland range.

We decided to return to Bryce early the next morning to watch the sunrise over the canyon. Since it was about an hour away, we were up and out early. Our hosts warned us to be careful because a lot of deer would be along the road. We all watched for wildlife as we drove in the dark to Bryce Canyon.

We hiked to Sunrise Point which provided the best view. It was a cold morning, so we were bundled with as many layers of clothes as we had. Watching the sun come up was beautiful. The sun glowed orange through the cloud banks. When the sun popped over the mountain tops it illuminated the canyon hoodoos in a brilliant orange. The hoodoos threw shadows against the canyon walls. It was a magnificent show.

We drove back to the park entrance to have a hearty breakfast buffet since our plan was to hike trails for the rest of the day. It also gave us a chance to warm up and shop for postcards and mail them to family.

After breakfast, we started our hike on the Peek-a-Boo Loop trail. The trail was wide and also used for horses. It was well maintained by the park service. That trail offered views of The Cathedral area with intricate hoodoo formations that were tall and slender. It looked like they could fall at any moment, yet would most likely stand for centuries.

It was an environment with little vegetation. The trail narrowed dramatically. We passed through a huge arch, which I almost missed because there was so much to look at including where I was placing my feet. Rain started to fall before we finished the hike which made the walk out challenging. The sandstone became slick as thunder began to boom closer and a small amount of hail fell. I thought about the warning of flash floods. We took cover under some overhanging rocks before completing the hike.

That night we discussed what to do on our final day in the area. The girls surprised me by suggesting we make the drive to the North Rim of the Grand Canyon. They had all been to the South Rim. I had never been to the Grand Canyon and was excited to have the opportunity to do so. I had seen a segment on CBS Sunday Morning on the North Rim, but never dreamed I would get to see it on this trip.

It was quite a drive, but we still arrived at the North Rim Visitor's Center mid-morning. We watched their video about the park and toured the visitor center to learn about the formation of the Grand Canyon. We made our way to Angel Point.

That slender trail overlooking the canyon offered views on both sides down to the base of the Colorado River. The point at the end of the trail had 360 degree views of the Grand Canyon. It was hard to find words to describe the incredible formations. It was breathtaking and unimaginable that a small river and water erosion could have formed it over millions of years.

We wanted to take a picture all together, but it was too crowded at the point. On the way back up the trail we found a small area and lined up one in front of the other leaning out so each of our faces could be seen with the Canyon surrounding us. A fellow traveler agreed to take our picture. It remains one of my favorite.

Near the visitor center, there were small rustic cabins scattered around a central lodge. The original 1928 Grand Lodge, built with native stone and timber, burned down. It was rebuilt in 1936 with the original stone and a modified smaller square footage. It sat on the edge of the canyon and included a restaurant, sitting area, porches and a meeting space.

There are many historical pictures and mementos in the main lobby. The most memorable for me was a statue of Brighty, the burro, who supposedly hauled materials to help build the lodge. We were to rub his nose for good luck before hiking in the canyon. His nose was so polished from rubs it shone.

Cloudsplitter insisted that I had to do at least a small portion of a hike into the Grand Canyon. The trail we picked was also used for mule riders, but I figured not many would be on the trail because the day threatened rain. I was so wrong. As we started out on the North Kaibab Trail we passed a large wood framed stand of water faucets. I thought, why are there so many water faucets!

The trail literally dropped off the side of the canyon and got narrower the deeper we went. Mule droppings were everywhere. I stepped delicately around them at first trying to keep my boots clean. At some point, I laughingly gave that up and just concentrated on my step placement. Cloudsplitter was moving downward like a mountain goat, but I paused frequently to take in the scenery. A light mist began to fall which made the mule droppings softer and the trail rocks more slippery.

That was as far as Thunderfoot and Runningbehind went. I

continued to the mile marker, and waited for a line of mules to pass. I stepped to the edge of the trail with the riders passing inches from me. There was no way I would have ridden a mule. The mules were slipping on the rocks as they scrambled to find secure footing. I will never forget some of the terrified faces I saw on the riders as they leaned back as far as they could to help the mules with balance. I wanted to laugh, but felt sorry for them, too.

I caught up with the mules and Cloudsplitter at a tunnel dug into the rock wall just as a soft rain began to fall. I was grateful when Cloudsplitter told me we should go back. I put on my rain poncho, rested a few minutes, then we started back up the trail.

Cloudsplitter would get ahead of me and then wait. Finally, I waved her to go on at her own pace. The trail became awash in mule dung. I had to move carefully and slowly. The rain intensified and became a downpour. I was not sight-seeing anymore. It took all I had to put each foot firmly on the ground and keep moving upward. I laughed at my awkwardness and prayed that I would not fall down into the wet, squishy dung.

We had a long ride back to the cabin. No one would appreciate my bringing manure along. I finally made it to the top with boots covered in slimy mule dung. It was then that I understood why the bank of faucets was there.

I washed off my boots to the best of my ability without a rag or brush as the rain poured over me. I could see the others were warm and dry in the car as I approached the parking lot.

I dropped to my knees and pseudo-kissed the ground before climbing into the car. Thunderfoot was the only one who saw it and was laughing as I opened the door. Most would not have attempted that hike with the weather conditions, but I was grateful to have had that unique and hilarious memory.

All I wanted was a warm shower at the cabin. We packed our bags that evening as we were leaving in the morning. I slept well in my bunk bed and heard no one else move all night. Come morning, we were all sad to leave our lovely cabin, Happy Ours, and our sweet hosts, Dave and Karren. Our destination was Las Vegas to spend the night and fly out early the following day.

En route, we made a stop at The Valley of Fire State Park. In the area was red Aztec sandstone from the Jurassic period. We hiked to a section of 2,500 year old petroglyphs thought to be made by the Basketmaker culture. Petroglyphs are prehistoric rock drawings. No one really knows why they were made. Later drawings from the Pueblo Indian time frame were thought to be used for communication. As the sun set, the surrounding mountains began to have an orange glow. The name of the park then became obvious.

I know many love Las Vegas. The activities and crowds energize them. We went to the casino in our hotel, but did not bother playing any machines. We walked the main street, but the crowds were overwhelming to me. Give me nature over this type of civilization.

We all went to the airport together early in the morning. Runningbehind had a later flight out. We said our goodbyes and headed to our gates. We found out later that Runningbehind played slots when she got bored waiting for her flight. She won a nice little jackpot.

I was glad to get home, but was already eager to visit another area of our beautiful country next year.

Chapter Twelve

North Cascades National Park, Washington —2012

Stehekin

Betsy Campbell, AKA Cloudsplitter

O f all the many wonderful parks and places that we have traveled, Stehekin sticks out in my mind as one of the most peaceful and spiritual. To begin with, the only way to get there was by hiking, float plane or boat.

The Pacific Crest Trail is 2,650 miles long running from

Mexico to Canada. It runs through California, Oregon and North Cascades National Park, Washington, about 12 miles from the village of Stehekin. We weren't doing the Pacific Crest Trail on this journey, but had lesser and more relaxing goals in mind. The tiny wilderness town of Stehekin and its environs was our destination. We chose the fast, scenic boat ride, which also offered us a guided tour of the lake's history, geology and beauty.

On August 14, 2012, Thunderfoot, Runningbehind and I landed in Seattle and were picked up by Wisdomwalk. We drove to the town of Chelan in her Prius which was perfect for the four of us. We spent that evening exploring the town, which sat at the head of Chelan Lake.

Even though Wisdomwalk lived in Washington, this was all new territory for her, too. The next morning, we headed down to the The Lady of the Lake Boat Dock where we would catch the ferry, *Lady Express*. That was the jump off point to get to Stehekin.

This glacially formed lake was 1,500 feet deep, the largest lake in Washington and the third deepest in the United States. There are two ferries that run from the town of Chelan to Stehekin, which was approximately a 50 mile long journey. *Lady II* was a leisurely run of four hours and *Lady Express* took two-and-one-half hours. We opted for the *Express*.

Thunderfoot has a problem with motion sickness and made a habit of never going on a boat. But the size of the ferry and the fact that it was just a two-and-one-half hour long trip had her in agreement to go. Taking the leisurely *Lady II* was not an option for her.

It wasn't until the boat was almost fully loaded and ready to go that Thunderfoot made her move off the dock. With determination, she joined us aboard *Lady Express* along with other visitors, sightseers and through-hikers. We were on our way to Stehekin.

It was a beautiful summer day and the boat cruised at a comfortable speed. Even Thunderfoot felt comfortable. We had great views of the rocky steep hills on either side of the lake.

While we were out of the harbor, but still close to shore, we were surrounded by what seemed like millions of boats of all sizes, along with jet skis zooming and zigzagging back and forth in front of the ferry. As the ferry advanced forward, the boats took up the space behind our vessel. They crisscrossed each other barely missing a collision. From our lofty perch it looked like shear madness, not to mention dangerous. We were informed that it was a daily occurrence here, especially in the summer.

There were very few places to stay. We rented two rooms at the North Cascade Lodge of Stehekin located right on the shore where the boats dock. Originally another friend was planning on coming with us. Wisdomwalk and I were going to stay in a camping area.

Two days before we left for Washington, the friend cancelled which gave Wisdomwalk and me a room at the inn. That was quite an upgrade as we now had a private bath and two comfy beds. Score! Her cancelation, albeit late, did come in time for us to leave all our camping gear at home.

When we arrived at the dock in Stehekin, a sign welcomed us to the Lake Chelan National Recreation Area in North Cascade National Park. The water was crystal clear and inviting, but once tested, was very cold. The North Cascade Lodge was straight in front of us. It looked welcoming and cozy and I was glad that we would be sleeping inside. It also looked like it was just about the only other building around.

We checked in and had two delightful upstairs rooms at the end of the hall across from each other. That was a perfect set up for us. We could leave our doors open and have a conversation between our rooms.

We had the afternoon to let the true meaning of Stehekin settle in our souls. There were two vintage red buses that took us to the far reaches of the area which was a 15 mile ride to High Bridge. Other than that, the options were walking or rental bikes.

There were a few private vehicles that were freighted over on a barge for the season. Not knowing anyone with a car, we set off walking. We even needed to walk to rent a bike, but for us that was half the fun. There was no cell phone service and only one satellite phone. We needed to wait patiently to use the phone with no guarantee that our call would go through. Forget about TV. We were out there.

We strolled down the road without any specific destination in mind and came upon a small outdoor cathedral. It consisted of a large wooden cross and several benches made from logs all overlooking Lake Chelan. It was called Groseclose Meditation Site and someone had carved "Be still and know I am God" into the logs. Its simplicity struck me. We seem to think that bigger is better, but this tiny open-air chapel seemed like it was just perfect. We sat down for a few minutes, each with our own thoughts and feelings.

We stopped at the Old Stehekin School House which was a real log cabin with fold-down wooden desks and old equipment. It was now a museum, but was once the original school. There were several items that brought our memories back to yesteryear. They even had an old crank mimeograph machine, the kind that would turn your hands blue if you were lucky enough to have your teacher pick you to assist in the printing.

Next we checked out the Paul Bunyon Table which again was made of logs—really, really, big logs. The table was at least six feet across and the tabletop was eight to 10 inches thick. The benches were half logs and we could just get our arms on the table while sitting. It really made me feel like a little kid that hadn't yet grown up enough to fit the adult's table.

We had read about a large organic garden that was in Stehekin and were excited to visit it. Both Wisdomwalk and I had worked at Rosaly's Garden, an organic farm in New Hampshire.

Wisdomwalk had a wonderful garden at her house in Washington that was thriving with innumerable veggies and fruits. We were ready to check out that garden. Gardening was a serious challenge in Florida and going organic was more like growing plants for bugs to munch on healthily. When we came upon the garden the gate was closed, so we put it on the docket for the next day.

Hunger got to us, especially after sitting at the Paul Bunyon Table with no food. We headed back to have supper at the restaurant at the Stehekin Landing. The food was good and seeing as we saw no other options, we really enjoyed the vittles.

On the way back to our room we did pass the Purple Paint Campground that Wisdomwalk and I would have been sleeping in and again, I had a moment of thankfulness to our friend that had to cancel. It did look like fun and several hikers were staying there, but I know how hard the ground can be as you get older and was appreciative that we would have a bed that evening.

We awoke to another cloudless, beautiful day. Our morning destination was the Stehekin Pastry Company which was about two miles down the road. At one-and-one-half miles we came again to the organic garden that was owned by Karl Gaskill, a gregarious gardener. Breakfast had to wait.

His garden was magnificent and bursting with flowers, fruit and vegetables bigger than I had seen in a long time. The kale row was long and wide and loaded with healthy looking kale that came up to my knee. Karl was barefoot and happy to talk to everyone that stopped by.

When asked how he made his veggies grow so well, he replied that he had bees for pollination and goats that provided plenty of manure. Along with the kelp and a gravity flow creek for irrigation, the garden thrived. His industrious goats also produced milk for cheese making. He had picked a southern exposure for his acre garden and the heat reflected off the rock bluffs that lined the garden in the back making for optimum growing conditions. And, of course, there was a never-ending supply of water during dry spells.

All that yummy food made us remember our original destination, so we said our goodbyes and headed down the road. After walking the road with shady woods on both sides, we could see a quaint building coming into view. It was in fact the legendary Stehekin Pastry Company and we could hardly wait. I thought, *a slightly stale plastic wrapped pastry sounded great!*

What greeted us as we entered was a real pastry shop with aromas to match and a glass case filled with fresh baked goodies. They had freshly made soups, and incredibly, if not almost impossibly, for it was in the middle of nowhere, deli sandwiches on homemade bread, pizza, salad and ice cream. This was something out of a dream.

Had this been in New York City it would have been a feat to get served, but fortunately there were just a handful of people. Most likely that was a crowd for the pastry shop as everyone there had to arrive by bike, bus or foot.

At the pastry shop we met a father and his two young sons who sailed their 18 foot boat from Chelan to Stehekin. They built the boat together and this was its maiden voyage. We had an interesting chat with the boys about their adventures, but soon turned our attention back to food.

One bite and we knew this would be our morning or lunch

ritual. Stress always has a way of sneaking in, even in the middle of euphoria, and I struggled with the thought of not having enough time on our last day to walk down to the bakery, eat and walk back to catch the boat back to Chelan. Pack the night before, perhaps?

Well that was in five days and I managed to put it out of my mind and enjoy the now. I'd worry about that tomorrow.

We found the Stehekin Pastry Company had three fully equipped cabins for rent. They also would pick you up at the dock in a car. It didn't make much sense to us to have a cabin with a kitchen once we found the Stehekin Pastry Company. No point in cooking when we had such a wonderful place to eat. We also knew where all the great veggies were coming from.

Other than the bakery, the *piece de resistance* of Stehekin was Rainbow Falls. That gorgeous multi-tiered waterfall cascades 312 feet in the upper section. Including the lower tier, Rainbow Falls was 392 feet to where it flows from Rainbow Creek eventually making its way to Chelan Lake. There was thankfully, a healthy flow to the falls while we were there. Magnificent barely describes it and we soon dubbed it Spirit Falls.

At the bottom it roared and threw mist with prism colors billowing into the air. I was sure we were not supposed to climb down to the bottom of the splash pool, but over the log fence Wisdomwalk and I went, getting soaking wet as we neared the bottom. The pounding and force of the water kept us at a respectful distance. We were standing right in the center of a beautiful rainbow created by the falls.

Later, we hiked the Purple Creek Trail which started just behind North Cascade Lodge. It is a beautiful trail. Unfortunately, it was in an area of an old burn. Past fires had ravaged that area, but we could see it was slowly recovering. Still, it was lovely having the sun filter through the blackened trees. There were plenty of deer munching on the new green grass and the young plants growing on the forest floor.

At three miles we came to an open boulder area that had gorgeous views looking down on the blue, blue lake and surrounding mountains. We soon made it past the burned area to the natural woods and enjoyed the rest of the hike.

One evening we took the red shuttle bus nine miles up Stehekin Valley Road to the Stehekin Valley Ranch for supper. That was a great rustic ranch nestled in a valley that offered tent and ranch cabins. The main building serves meals for all the guests and provides extra electrical power for the tent cabins.

The land was owned by the Courtney family since the 1950's and was developed into a guest ranch in 1983. The ranch was mostly run on solar power with battery storage, along with a fossil fuel generator. We feasted on the delicious meal served in a room with large glass windows overlooking the scenery, and just like all the rest of Stehekin, it was beautiful.

The next day we took the red shuttle bus again, this time to High Bridge at the end of the road. High Bridge was nothing more than a destination by the river with a campground and ranger cabin. The buses run the 12 miles from the dock at Stehekin Landing stopping and turning back at the bridge that crossed over the Stehekin River.

The bridge had washed out several years ago and was now a foot bridge for hikers. High Bridge connected many trails including the Pacific Crest Trail which we wanted to check out. Stehekin was the last town on the Pacific Crest Trail before it crossed the Canadian border. A lot of through-hikers catch the shuttle bus into Stehekin for some rest and relaxation before the push to Canada.

The Stehekin River was a mighty river of turquoise water tumbling over rocks and downed trees. Its beauty and fierceness lend a fine juxtaposition that was so prevalent in the area. On the one hand the beauty was so incredibly breathtaking, while on the other hand so dangerous and potentially life threatening. Apparently, people can kayak the lower section of the river, but at this location it didn't look remotely possible to me.

We decided to hike the Agnes Gorge Trail which follows along the Stehekin River being careful to time it so we could meet the last returning bus of the day. Soon Wisdomwalk and I were ahead of Runningbehind and Thunderfoot as Thunderfoot was stopping to videotape the scenery.

The roar of the river made it difficult to hear much around us, and it was hard not to look down the gorge and appreciate its power. Wisdomwalk and I turned back at the allotted time and did not pass them on the way back. When we got to the bridge they were not there. We had 20 minutes to go before the bus arrived. What surprised us was the fact that we didn't pass them on the way back and we only went out and back, with no side trips.

With 10 minutes to go, Wisdomwalk went back up the trail while I stayed to ask the driver to wait. Hopefully he would. I anxiously waited as the bus arrival time became five minutes, then three minutes. With one minute left, I saw all three cheerily coming down the trail.

"Where did you go?" I asked with a little more anxiety than they exhibited.

"We stopped to enjoy the river," chimed Runningbehind.

"Boy, that was so beautiful!" added Thunderfoot.

A few minutes later (fortunately not on time) the bus pulled up and we got on board. I marveled that I was the only one that seemed to be worried about missing the bus, but that was the magic of Stehekin. It was, after all, only a 12 mile walk back to our rooms.

The next day we took a ranger-led tour of Buckner Orchard. The Buckner Homestead had many historic structures including the oldest building in the valley. The apple orchard is still operational and was originally irrigated by hand-dug ditches, and it still is. In 1974, it was listed on the National Register of Historical Places and is now run by the Park Service.

While standing in the orchard we saw a black bear amongst the apple trees. He didn't seem to mind the Ranger talking and we got great pictures of him. He was not in any rush and just hung out with us, no doubt mostly interested in the dropped apples. It was a treat for us to watch him.

When we got back to the landing a few people were

swimming. Runningbehind and Wisdomwalk were the only ones that brought bathing suits. We decided to test the waters. I had to swim in my clothes. It was very cold, but it was so clear and beautiful that we managed to get in. There was a huge log about 36 inches in diameter tied in the deep water most likely to help stop the ferries should the need arise. Wisdomwalk and I swam out to the log and with great effort managed to get on top of it. No easy feat.

Finally, Runningbehind decided to come in and someone lent her a rubber blow up raft. Runningbehind became one with it, floating in the cold, clear Stehekin water. It felt like we were "taking the waters" and there just might have been some youthful qualities to it, too. While we were in the lake, all our cares seemed to vanish. We felt so rejuvenated afterwards.

Of course, we couldn't stay away from Rainbow Falls. The next day we found ourselves at the overlook only this time, Thunderfoot and Runningbehind climbed over the fence and headed down to the splash pool.

Their shirts were billowing with the force of the falls and the mist was chilling them down. It's amazing the power the falls had on us. Here we had perfectly law-abiding mature women hopping fences and doing possibly very dangerous stuff. That time we were not alone at the overlook, and once Runningbehind and Thunderfoot came back, two gentlemen gave it a try. I am sure they loved it.

We were walking down Stehekin Road one afternoon coming back from a hike when a pickup truck drove up to us.

Seeing any vehicle on the road was an unusual happening. The driver asked where we were going, and we told him we were staying at the North Cascade Lodge. He said, "Hop in the back, I'm going to the dock." All four of us threw in our daypacks and climbed in the back. We shouldn't have been surprised by their kindness; they were just used to tired hikers.

We met a very nice young fellow working at the Lodge as a handy man/maid. He had the following day off and was taking the boat to the town of Chelan. He offered us the use of his bike for that day. It was parked out back, unlocked, of course, so we rented three more. That day we got to see a lot more of Stehekin with our wheels.

We hadn't quite planned our trip for optimum alignment with the stars. We didn't know how much wide-open sky there was above Chelan Lake. Also, it turned out Stehekin had some of the darkest skies in Washington. It was pitch black each evening.

We missed the Perseides Meteor Showers by about a week and can only guess how spectacular it must have been in Stehekin. We did luck out with a ranger led evening astronomy talk and telescope viewing on the shore of the lake. The ranger also had a laser light that he could shine in the sky to point out all the constellations, clusters and nebulas. He even showed us the space station as it made its way across the black sky.

It was awesome and something I hadn't really thought about since I was much younger, even though the sky is always right above me every day and night. All was not lost though, we did see a few falling stars.

The year before, our fellow Happy Hiker friend, Doris Graham, Dustcatcher, died from a completely unexpected aneurism. We wanted to take a few moments while in Stehekin to reflect on her life. It would be nothing fancy, just a few words in honor of her. On the McGregor Trail we came to a beautiful overview of the lake and glaciered mountains. Runningbehind asked if this would be a good spot. It was, but we decided to go back to Rainbow Falls, our Spirit Falls. There, we reminisced about Dustcatcher to the grandeur of the falls and it seemed appropriate. We summed up our celebration of Dustcatcher's life with John Muir's wonderful quote which we knew she would appreciate:

"Climb the mountains and get their good tidings.

Nature's peace will flow into you as sunshine flows into trees.

The wind will blow their own freshness into you, and the storms their energy

While cares will drop away from you like the leaves of autumn."

While on our hike on the McGregor Trail, Wisdomwalk and I took the lead. Thunderfoot and Runningbehind were a little behind us. Suddenly, three deer came charging towards us. It was a doe and her two fawns. The young ones, upon seeing us, ran in different directions. The mom nearly ran into us, but veered off at the last minute. We soon found out why. Lumbering up the hill was a black bear. Fortunately, he took off once he noticed us.

Thank goodness we scared him because he sure scared us! We hoped the mom and babies would rejoin each other soon.

Runningbehind and I made our last stroll to the satellite phone. Timing was everything. As this was the only way to communicate with the folks back home, it was very busy. It was best to stand in line because if we left to go do something else and check back later, our spot was quickly filled. Fortunately, most everyone knew that and was kind enough to keep their conversations short. There wasn't any privacy anyway.

It was just a phone attached to the outside of a building and whoever was lucky enough to be on the phone was surrounded by several people standing nearby listening. It was a little inconvenient, but it seemed such a small price to pay for all the beauty around us.

We met a girl that was hiking the whole Pacific Crest Trail solo. She had stopped in Stehekin to recharge her batteries, literally and figuratively. She joined us for supper and regaled us with her adventures thus far. She was planning on staying a day or two and then heading back on the trail to Canada. It was great to hear her tale, but she was quite a bit younger and none of us mentioned about trying it ourselves.

If nothing else, the Stehekin life was a great reminder of how simple life could be. We were most fortunate to have wonderful weather the whole time we were there. If it had been raining, I am sure we wouldn't have been so enthralled, but it was gorgeous each day to the point of being ideal.

Or perhaps, that was just the magic of the place. Every

day we walked by the outdoor chapel; by the organic garden, knowing Karl Gaskell, wasn't wearing any shoes; our Spirit Falls; the unbelievable pastry shop in the middle of nowhere; the friendly hikers and the beautiful crystal-clear blue of Lake Chelan. The Spirit was there for certain. It's a little bit closer to heaven in Stehekin. It was just right.

I never did get to the Stehekin Pastry Company the morning of our last day, but my soul was full. As we watched Stehekin grow smaller and smaller from the deck of the *Lady Express*, we knew we were touched by the magic of the place. There was a part of each of us that would not be making the journey home.

Chapter Thirteen

Adirondack Mountains, New York —2013

Vermont

Nancy Fetzer, AKA Runswithdogs

The July trip to Lake Placid, New York, was my initiation into the Happy Hikers. After listening to all of their past adventures, I was happy to give it a try. My feelings were mixed as I drove from Pennsylvania to the Adirondack Mountains. I was nervous about fitting in as I am pretty much a loner, so there was apprehension as well as anticipation. The fact that I

Nancy Fetzer, AKA Runswithdogs

could drive and not fly was the most enticing part of this trip. I prefer driving my car any day over flying and as it turned out the drive was beautiful.

I was the first to arrive at the hostel in Lake Placid which was aptly named, Lake Placid Hostel. I met the owner, John, and started walking down the road in the direction Thunderfoot, Blueridgebelle, Runningbehind and my sister, Cloudsplitter, would be arriving. They all flew into Burlington, Vermont, and were driving a rental car west to the Adirondacks.

Sure enough, I ran into them a short way down the road. We checked in and my time as a Happy Hiker began. Runningbehind presented me with a tee shirt with my new trail name on it— Runswithdogs. It was now official.

Speaking of Runningbehind, she confided in us that she had mistakenly booked her flight at 6:00 p.m. instead of 6:00 a.m. She didn't know that until she got to the airport 13 hours early. Talk about being on time! Runningbehind, fortunately, got another flight, but confessed that she almost canceled coming. With all that, she still wasn't the last to arrive which made her feel a little better. Blueridgebelle missed her connecting flight because a flight attendant overslept. These fascinating tales are one of the reasons I don't like to fly.

As luck would have it, we were the only guests at the hostel for our first days, so we got to share two bathrooms (and possibly we used all four). We had three sets of bunk beds in one room. The breakfasts were made by our host, John, and were truly amazing. His wife was out of town, so he did all the prep, cooking and cleaning by himself. He wore a white apron each day and it really did become him.

Each breakfast consisted of oatmeal, organic cornbread, eggs anyway we wanted, all made by John. I brought real Pennsylvania maple syrup with me. Once John realized this, he was happy to add pancakes to his repertoire.

For the next four days, we enjoyed his excellent meals and his wealth of information. After serving, he would retreat to the kitchen, but after a day or two we got him to join us at the breakfast table.

We decided to hike around the lake downtown, which we thought was Lake Placid. It turned out to be Mirror Lake, a smaller sister lake. While navigating the path, we came across a lady from the area who knew John.

She recommended that we consider hiking Cascade Mountain and said of all the mountains in the area it was the "best bang for the buck." We decided to take the local's advice and the next day we headed for Cascade.

Cascade Mountain was one of the Adirondack's 46 high peaks with an elevation of 4,098 feet. It was rated two out of a one to seven difficulty rating, so it sounded like a good one to start with.

Cloudsplitter and I soon were ahead of the girls hiking a little faster than they were. I asked her if we should wait for the others, but she said they all climb at their own speed. However, we could stop and wait for them any time. As a newbie, I wanted to get all the rules down pat. Normally, I just go for the top, but stopping to eat, drink and exchange interesting happenings with the group did provide insights that I would probably have missed otherwise. Also, it let me enjoy the beauty around me more than just studying the path.

Even though my sister and I had been hiking together most of our lives, it was quite challenging near the top of Cascade. Above the tree line, it was all exposed boulders with a bit of scrambling. We made it to the top, which had a dramatic 360 degree view, and found a spot which overlooked the trail, so we could watch for the girls. The day was sunny with few clouds and wonderful views.

After we all had lunch together at the top, we headed back down. On the way, we ran into an older couple who were trying to get over one of the boulders. First the husband was trying to push his wife up from the bottom of the rock and then he got on top of the rock and tried pulling her up with his hiking pole.

She appeared to be getting nervous and having second thoughts about going to the top, but he wanted her to make it for the view. We offered our help and while he was on top of the boulder giving her a hand, we were boosting her up from the bottom. In two seconds, she was up. They were grateful and thanked us and we assured her it was the last big boulder.

We were at the bottom of the mountain waiting for the girls when we saw the couple again. They thanked us and drove off to Keene. Blueridgebelle was next down which was good as she had the key to the car. A short time later, the same couple drove up beside us. They had a six pack of beer and a bottle opener in thanks for the help. Laurie offered to pay, but they refused. Laurie said, "We will pay it forward." Off they went, and we enjoyed an *après* hiking beer.

To this day, I have that opener on my key chain, because one thing worse than not having a beer is to have one without an opener.

The next days were rainy, so we toured Whiteface Lodge and Adirondack Lodge. I should mention that "toured" was a bit of a misnomer. We actually "snooped" around the lodges, but fortunately no one could tell the snoops from the lodgers. Those majestic Adirondack lodges were simply gorgeous, but I still liked our hostel best. Perhaps, we would stay in one of the lodges another time.

We drove up to Adirondack Loj to see picturesque Heart Lake and decided to hike up to Marcy Dam regardless of the rainy weather. When we got to the ranger station, we learned the dam had been destroyed by Hurricane Irene in 2011. It was totally different from when Cloudsplitter and Thunderfoot had climbed Mt. Marcy years before. The bridge that crossed the river was gone and there was no clear way to get to the other side at that point. The Adirondack Park Agency, or the powers that be, decided not to rebuild the dam, but let the area go wild as it had been originally.

At night, all snug in our bunks, Thunderfoot read to us from her book, *Farmer Boy,* at Cloudsplitter's request. Cloudsplitter was asleep in five minutes. The rest of us listened.

The next day John offered to take us mushroom gathering.

He assured us that he knew the correct ones to eat and he would cook them for our next breakfast. It sounded tempting, but we decided to hike Whiteface Mountain instead. We told him that if we got back in time we would love to go. Apparently, the rain they were having was great for mushroom growing.

We drove up Whiteface Mountain to the stone castle near the top. There were two ways to get to the summit. One was to walk up a path to the top or take a 27 story elevator. We chose the elevator and walked through a long tunnel drilled through the rock.

We got in the elevator and people kept coming in until we were tightly packed like sardines. Literally, no one would be able to sit down should something go wrong (Definitely not good for claustrophobics). Of course, nothing went wrong and within a few moments we were out in the fresh air at the top.

That was an experience all by itself. None of us wanted to ride the elevator back down. We had a picnic at the top enjoying the beautiful view of the Adirondack Mountains and then hiked down to the car.

On the way back to the hostel we passed an A&W Root Beer stand and decided to stop. While sipping our root beer, we reminisced about how simple life used to be. None of us had had a root beer in years, and boy was it delicious. We didn't get back in time for mushroom hunting.

The next morning we had a mushroom-less breakfast. We all thanked John for his hospitality, bid him goodbye and headed to Vermont. (Whoopee, now we were talking). Vermont was my favorite state in the Union and we were headed there. We had to take the same ferry across Lake Champlain the girls had taken only days before. As they were saying goodbye to New York, I was saying hello to Vermont.

Our first stop was at the original Ben & Jerry's in Stowe for ice cream. It was packed with people, but we finally got our cones. Next stop was the Von Trapp Lodge also in Stowe. We had to check out the restroom, of course, and I should tell you, that I have been in a lot of mighty fine bathrooms. I do like my restrooms grand and stately.

We arrived at the base of Mt. Mansfield, Vermont's highest mountain, late in the day just before 4:00 p.m. Unfortunately, that was when they lock the gate for the evening. They let us go up, but we would have to retrieve the key from the base hotel when we got down. Laurie drove us to the upper parking lot. We were the only ones there other than a couple that was headed back down.

Mt. Mansfield's profile was supposed to resemble a reclining man's head with the forehead, nose and chin. We started our hike to the summit (the chin). Rain was threatening and the view with the dark clouds was breathtaking. At the summit, we were surrounded by clouds and it seemed like we could reach out and touch them. We started back down and were passed by Blueridgebelle who was making the fastest descent ever. We could see her off in the distance getting smaller and smaller. The clouds were getting black, but were lit beautifully by the setting sun. We made it down cold but dry.

We were off to Injun Joe's Cabins in Danville, and on our way stopped in a small town at what looked like the only restaurant there. It was called Marshfield Bakery and Café and fortunately was still open. It consisted of a counter and just a few tables.

The owner was a very friendly character who was talking to everyone in the place including us. We ended up having a terrific meal with everyone joining in the conversation. It made us feel like we were invited guests. We asked for directions and arrived at Injun Joe's at 10:30 p.m.

Cloudsplitter and I went to register and had to wait quite awhile for the elderly owner to come. She was a little grumpy at that late hour and said she thought we were no shows. We apologized, and she sweetened up and gave us the keys to our cabins.

Wow, those were cute little cabins. They were just my cup of tea. There was barely enough room to walk in between our twin beds, but I didn't care. It was a real cabin in Vermont. Cloudsplitter's and my beds were very comfortable.

We found out the next morning that Thunderfoot was not as lucky. Hers was uncomfortable and Runningbehind and Blueridgebelle, who were sharing a double, kept rolling into the center. I'm sure they don't have quite the same wonderful feelings about Vermont cabins as I do.

In the morning, we walked down the road to Joe's Lake Store which pretty much was the only game in town (Correction, the only game in town). We sat down at the counter along with a few men that were there and were introduced to the waitress, Evelyn. Evelyn literally did it all. She was cook, server, dishwasher, store clerk and chatted away to her customers who, other than us, were all regulars. We didn't go unnoticed though, as we were the only five females there other than Evelyn.

Cloudsplitter had brought along her own tea bag, so I asked Evelyn if she had any hot water.

She replied, "Of course we do, this is a restaurant."

We were thinking about pancakes, so we asked Evelyn if she had any real maple syrup.

She stopped in front of us, put her hand on her hip and said, "You girls ask the silliest questions. Of course, we do. This is Vermont and if you go to a restaurant in Vermont and they don't have real maple syrup, you need to walk out."

Evelyn was a sassy one and we all enjoyed her banter.

Next stop was Lake Willoughby. It was long overdue for Cloudsplitter and me, as an old friend of ours loved the lake, mentioned it frequently and then named his son after it. It was beautiful and sat between two mountains that appeared to rise right on the shore.

We stopped at the Willoughby Inn and did our usual snooping. We decided to climb Mt. Pisgah, one of the mountains that graced the lake. It started to pour, and those of us who weren't prepared, found any kind of protection we could find, i.e. trash bags. They sure do come in handy and are now our standard pack gear!

We made it to the top through the intermittent rain and

enjoyed the spectacular views of the lake down below. By the time we made it to the bottom, the rain had completely stopped.

After dinner at McAllister's Tavern, we went back home to Injun Joes! All night long the loons serenaded us. Cloudsplitter, who loves loons slept through most of it, but I stayed awake and listened to their lovely mournful sound—I'm pretty sure there was a full moon, too!

Next morning, we had to see Evelyn again. We didn't want to miss out on the fun interaction, good food, hot water and real maple syrup. We shared our adventures with her and we learned a lot more about the area and that multi-talented lady. When she wasn't working in the diner, she was working on a farm. We just loved that sassy lassie.

We headed next to Cabot where Cloudsplitter had heard from a lady in Punta Gorda, Florida, that there was a beautiful secluded pond that she used to swim in as a child. She had given Cloudsplitter directions and we finally found it after many turnarounds.

It was indeed a very pristine and undeveloped pond. A fellow was burning brush in a nearby field and he ventured towards us. After we talked a little while, he invited us to meet his wife over by the burn pile. She, like her husband, was a delightful Vermonter. They had built their home just up the hill. He told us his son was visiting and we should all go up to the house and pretend that we were interested developers. We all thought it would be a great joke.

On their back porch, overlooking the surrounding

mountains, Blueridgebelle launched into her great sales pitch to their son, Mike. Within seconds, his smile left his face, and his body posture got more and more defensive. He folded his arms tightly and stood more erect. His face was stern. Blueridgebelle finished her spiel and smiled sweetly at him. He finally said, "You are not going to develop."

We all started to laugh, and he relaxed. We told him the real reason we were there, and he said, "Well, I didn't think you looked like developers." We surely didn't!

Once the pressure was off, Don and Marylou gave us a tour of their lovely home and the cabin they built to live in while they were building the main house, which was gorgeous. However, I was in love with the one room cabin. I do have a healthy appreciation for mansions, but small cabins, whether they are one room or two, have always made my heart skip. Their cabin was perfect!

In the end, Mike recommended a good hike nearby called Nichols Ledge. We said our farewells and followed his directions. It was a very nice hike to a ledge that offered a beautiful panoramic view of the valley below. It was lovely, and we knew Mike had truly forgiven us for our little prank.

We bought lunch at a small store in a nearby town and had a picnic on the shores of Osmore Pond in Groton State Forest. After lunch, we said goodbye to our buddies who were flying out of Burlington, while Cloudsplitter and I were driving back to New Hampshire.

We were feeling so sad about our friends' departure that

we had to hike around the lake to assuage our sorrow. When we got back to Osmore Pond and were getting ready to leave, we heard a loon echoing its haunting cry off the lake. It was a beautiful farewell song to my first adventure as Runswithdogs.

Chapter Fourteen

Shenandoah National Park, Virginia —2014

Nancy Fetzer, AKA Runswithdogs.

For many years the word Shenandoah has held a special place in my heart. There was the beautiful song by that name that was popular in my youth, but mostly my fond feelings come from the movie *Shenandoah* starring Jimmy Stewart. The young suitor of Jimmy Stewart's daughter comes to him to ask for her hand in marriage. He asks the eager young man, "Do you like her?"

The young man replies, "No sir, I love her."

Jimmy says, "No, no, do you like her?"

That one scene made a lasting impression on me and as the years rolled on, I found out how poignant it was. Like is longer lasting than love and a tough lesson to learn. Boy, was I surprised how much one could love Shenandoah the Park—or would that be like?

I missed the first day of our trip due to scheduling as I was flying from the backwoods of Pennsylvania. I have the pleasure of spending a few months each summer and fall at my friend Lou's house on a lake in Poyntelle, Pennsylvania. Its seclusion is one of the great things about it, but it does present minor challenges when traveling by plane. My flight to Charlottesville, Virginia, arrived at 10:16 p.m. (Sorry girls.)

Blueridgebelle drove her car from North Carolina to Charlottesville, so we wouldn't have to rent a car. She was the designated driver for this trip. The esteemed honor of being the driver goes to whomever has their car at our destination or is the youngest.

Blueridgebelle usually gets the job, but this time it was in her own car. The girls told me that when they got off the plane, Blueridgebelle was standing with all the Limo drivers holding a sign that said, "Happy Hikers".

By the time I got there Runningbehind, Thunderfoot, Blueridgebelle and my sister, Cloudsplitter, had already spent the previous night in our cabin and checked out the area. We had a cute log cabin called Camp Southern Comfort in the mountains just outside the park.

The cabin had two bedrooms on the main floor. Cloudsplitter and I had the whole finished cellar as our room which sported a ping pong table in the center. If we couldn't sleep, we could play a few games without waking the girls upstairs.

We were very cool in the cellar, but upstairs was stuffy, so the girls would put on the air conditioning. Unfortunately, this turned the already cool cellar into a frigid room. It took a little doing to get a balance of comfort in our Southern Comfort. We settled it by opening the door downstairs which did let in some warm August mountain air.

There was a strange contraption in the backyard. It was all metal and chains, none of us could figure out what it was. Later we learned that it was for Frisbee Golf and apparently, quite popular. One learns something new every day!

Next morning Cloudsplitter and I got up at 5:00 a.m. We decided to go for a walk rather than play ping pong. I wanted to see where we were as I had arrived in the dark.

It was lovely and I congratulated Cloudsplitter on another fine choice of accommodations. On our way back to the cabin Cloudsplitter found a tick attached to her ear. She got it off, but I know quite a few people that have had Lyme disease, so I was concerned and checked each day for changes in that area. There were none!

This was one of the rare times when we had our own

kitchen, so we had several meals at the cabin. Oatmeal is my breakfast of choice and it tasted great in the mountains. After breakfast we drove to Stony Man Mountain. The views on top of Stony Man were breathtaking with all the many soft shades of blues and grays of the rolling mountains. I worried about rattlesnakes, as I don't like snakes of any kind. Cloudsplitter assured me there weren't any and if there were, they would only be at the top.

Cloudsplitter, in her usual leader mode, led the way back down the trail. At the bottom I nearly stepped on a rattlesnake that Cloudsplitter had disturbed. It was a close call. We were just recovering from tick fear and now this.

The snake was heading off the trail slowly slithering his thick diamond body and rattles with him. Seeing as no one was hurt, we felt brave enough to take several pictures. I thanked my lucky stars and decided in the future not to rely on all of Cloudsplitter's "expertise".

A few months later, Runningbehind wrote this poem about the snake, immortalizing the fellow:

The Good, Good Snake

One lengthy rattler
Gliding through the grass,
Wanted to cross the trail
Where hikers were about to pass.

The creatures coming fast

Put fear inside his heart.
He quickly made a coil,
Not knowing which way to dart.

Strike ready as they approached,
"Oh! Runswithdogs," he said,
"So, I really do
Have nothing to dread."

"I'll respect your ways,
You respect mine.
Surely a way to live
For all of mankind."

Next day we drove a section of the Blue Ridge Parkway and had many photo ops: flowers, scenery, bears, mountains and even Mary's Tunnel through the rock, just to name a few.

We climbed the Mary's Rock Trail which led to, no surprise here, more beautiful views. At the summit of the trail is a huge boulder—Mary's Rock. This is quite a popular trail and there were a few people waiting to climb to the top of the rock for the best view. Whether on the boulder or not, it was a magnificent vista.

Hightop Mountain was our next hike and we met a group of "elder" hikers from Wintergreen, Virginia, who just happened to winter in Florida. This, of course, led to some interesting conversation. They also shared with us some of their "bests" in Shenandoah. We joined them for lunch on the ledges in the sunshine. Almost all the hikers we meet are friendly and gregarious. It was my experience that nice people hike—no matter what age!

We took many photos with our signature pink hats. Cloudsplitter bought the hats for everyone at Tractor Supply a few years ago. The color was bright pink and most likely because of the color, they were on sale. She bought them for the sun protection and not the color, but the color took.

I mentioned how nice we all looked in our "pinkitivity". Some of the hats have come and gone, but the pinkitivity of the hats remains the same and the new ones are always pink. Besides, we can really spot each other on the mountain trails.

That night we had supper at a café before going back to the cabin. We were wearing our T-shirts with our trail names on them. Runningbehind was cold and put on her jacket. We were waiting in line when some young fellows came in behind us. After a few minutes, one of the guys asked Runningbehind what her name was. Runningbehind turned around and with a surprised look she said timidly, "Cleo."

We knew he was asking about her trail name which he couldn't see because of her jacket. We laughed about it, chatting some more with the guys. He told Runningbehind that he would buy her dinner and of course she said, "No, no, that is nice, but totally not necessary." We shortly got our seats and thanked the guys.

Of course, once we were seated at our table, we teased Runningbehind unmercifully about being such a cougar! She still has it. And good to his word, the young man bought her dinner. The rest of us had to pay.

Our next excursion was the Rose River Falls Trail. This was a change of pace for us as we usually are looking for mountain hikes and expect to go up. This trail went down into a wooded, cool valley with waterfalls. We stopped to have a snack by the rushing river which we assumed was Rose River. As we had gone steadily downhill for this hike Thunderfoot, Runningbehind and Blueridgebelle decided to go back up before they went any further.

Cloudsplitter and I decided to go further on the Rose River Falls Loop Trail. We made the right decision. The river got larger and we had a few more miles of nonstop waterfalls and dramatic cascades, each more spectacular than the one before. The trail followed the river and was cool and shaded. There were huge boulders that we had to walk around, and you could barely comprehend how it was all formed so many years ago. Some of the balsic volcanic rock was approximately 400 to 800 million years old. That was a very interesting fact and almost an incomprehensible idea for my brain.

There were so many falls that it was hard not to stop and pose for pictures beside each one. I had an old camera and had to keep changing batteries. It was awesome and I don't think we even saw another person until we arrived at Dark Hollow Falls, which was one of the most hiked falls in the park.

Fortunately, it was late afternoon and only a few people were there. Unfortunately, we went up the trail to the Dark Hollow parking lot and still had a mile to go along the Skyline

Highway to get back to Blueridgebelle's car where the girls were waiting. We got our exercise that day.

We did a load of laundry back at the cabin only to discover that we didn't have enough hot water for showers. While waiting for the water to get warm, we watched Thunderfoot's video and pictures of the previous year's trip. She had written captions for some of the pictures which were very humorous. Slowly we all got clean.

After breakfast the following day we headed to Charlottesville to tour Thomas Jefferson's estate, Monticello. We toured the flower and vegetable gardens, house, slave quarters, tunnels, wine cellar, smokehouse and kitchen. It amazed me what they accomplished as their tools were so primitive in comparison to what we have today. The level of living was quite high for that time as Jefferson was such an innovative man.

We each took turns taking our picture with the bronze statue of Thomas Jefferson. We all stood beside it, but when it was Runningbehind's turn, she tucked her hand into his and it was adorable. Of course, he was unmoved by the gesture!

We got into Shenandoah National Park free via Runningbehind's Senior Park Pass. Luckily, I purchased one shortly thereafter as now the price has since increased significantly. The younger girls will just have to pay or stick with Runningbehind and me!

Every morning, Cloudsplitter and I got up early for a walk down the dirt road that led up to our cabin. It was a great way to escape the cold basement and warm up. One morning we weren't up fast enough and were awakened at 6 a.m. by Runningbehind's alarm. She was standing at the top of the stairs banging a cookie sheet with a spoon. Ugh, it was a terrible wake up.

I had heard about people doing such things, but I never expected it from Runningbehind. She seemed so nice, but there she was, banging away. We were headed to Old Rag Mountain and she wanted an early start.

Turns out this was the best hike. The weather couldn't have been more perfect, cool and clear. Old Rag is a popular, much hiked mountain with a boulder scramble at the top. At the overlook there were precariously balanced rocks everywhere. We came across a large group of high school cross-country runners and stepped off the trail for them as they ran by. (Now, there was a fit group.)

After we had some lunch with a view, Cloudsplitter and I went on a little further to see the famous Old Rag boulders. It was awesome but we opted not to do it. We still have some brains left. I was proud to hear Cloudsplitter say, "I no longer believe that I can't fall."

Of course, we couldn't leave without seeing the summer retreat of former president Herbert Hoover, called "Rapidan." It was a cloudy day when we set off on the lovely trail through the woods to Hoover Camp. When we arrived, it started to rain. No one was there and the buildings were locked. We ate lunch on the porch trying to get under the eaves out of the rain. It was a rustic peaceful getaway surrounded by gorgeous waterfalls and several buildings. We peeked in the windows as best we could. The rain let up, but our trip back was wet and tedious as it was very slippery.

Driving back to our cabin on the Skyline Parkway, we were treated to a different mood of Shenandoah. Each day the mountain vistas had been mostly sunshine and clouds. Due to the recent rain that had fallen, there was a thick fog passing through the mountains. It made for a dramatic, yet eerie scene, unlike any we had witnessed since we arrived.

On our last night, we cooked a dinner of quesadillas and had a surprise early birthday party for Thunderfoot. At the dinner table that evening Runningbehind said, "Say, we should really write a book about all our adventures." And right there, in our cabin, that night, the idea was born.

I was first to leave the next day and luckily the airport was close. But even though I was gone, I heard about copious amounts of food being thrown in the trash. As we are all interested in doing our part to conserve and Thunderfoot, Runningbehind and Cloudsplitter could not take anything on the plane, Blueridgebelle got stuck taking a lot of it. It was a great lesson though. Our new mantra was—never over buy— one that could be added to Cleo's "Rules for a Perfect Trip." (A wise woman indeed.)

Shenandoah meant so much more to me as I flew away. I loved and, more importantly, liked Shenandoah!

Chapter Fifteen

Twin Lake Village, New Hampshire —2015

Lake Sunapee

Nancy Fetzer, AKA Runswithdogs

Once again, I had the pleasure of driving my own car to our rendezvous spot in classic New London, New Hampshire. Not only that, but it was to a place that I knew quite well because my Uncle Bill had lived in the same town for many years.

What a surprise I had when I arrived at Twin Lake Village

and they showed me to our annex suite. Our annex had three bedrooms, three baths and a living room. We also had a dance hall downstairs below our suite with fireplace and piano. This was just like the dance hall in the movie *Dirty Dancing* and I wasn't sure if the movie hadn't been filmed here. It hadn't, but it was remarkably similar and set me in the mood. (Where was Patrick Swayze?)

Twin Lake Village was an all-inclusive family resort that was unpretentious while still being elegant. It was an old, white clapboard inn with a long covered front porch lined with multi colored rocking chairs beckoning me to sit.

It offered hotel rooms and cottages, along with three meals a day in their dining hall. Also included was their 9 hole par 3 golf course, clay tennis and shuffle board courts, a sandy beach on the lake and kayaks or rowboats. My Uncle had played golf here and knew the owner, so I had known about the place for many years. Now I was a guest.

I was the first to arrive. I had driven up from Pennsylvania and the girls were flying into Manchester and renting a car. Well, first come, first serve. I had the pleasure of choosing the room for Cloudsplitter and myself. It was a hard choice as they were all nice and with private baths.

Runningbehind and Blueridgebelle had arrived first in Manchester and went out to lunch in Hudson where Blueridgebelle used to live. Thunderfoot and Cloudsplitter had a three hour layover in Baltimore/Washington and were trying to get an earlier standby flight out. They only had room for one and Thunderfoot said to Cloudsplitter, "Don't you dare even think about leaving me here alone." They waited the full three hours.

When they arrived, I gave them the tour of our new home for the week. They were impressed and settled into their chosen bedrooms—minus one that I had picked.

We had been told that dress was casual for breakfast and lunch, but they suggested "to dress" for supper. We thought that meant not your hiking clothes. At our first supper we realized what they meant by dress.

Many ladies were in dresses and heels while the men were in suits. Oh my! We were shown to a table in a corner of an alcove. As it turned out, getting dressed up was optional, but jeans were not allowed. We were tucked away in our corner, so not too many people could see us anyway.

This table was designated ours for the duration of the week. The location of our reserved table might have been about our taste in clothes, but for us it was perfect to be in our nook. The staff, nevertheless, was professional to the point of not letting us know of our *faux pas*. (As a hiking group our jeans and tee shirts were our best dress.) However, we did hit a few secondhand clothing stores the next day.

The food was spectacular and there was plenty of it. For each meal we all filled out a personal menu including a choice of *hors d'oeuvre*, entree, fruit, salad, soup, drinks and dessert. Everything was fresh and delicious.

No limits either, which made it a jackpot for hungry

hikers. We made sure that we made every breakfast and supper, regardless of where we were hiking, even if we had to cut it short. Lunches we would miss, but fortunately for us, they happily provided a box lunch which included fruit, sandwich, dessert and a drink. We figured we could slum it for lunch.

We were quickly becoming spoiled, reliant, but grateful, wussy hikers. After breakfast every day, we picked up our individual paper bag lunches at the front desk and headed for the local mountains.

In spite of living in New Hampshire most of my life, I had never hiked Mt. Cardigan, 3,144 feet. It was a delightful hike with boulders and open views at the top. We all met at the top and had our great boxed lunches. The mountain was perfect for our first day hiking.

Cloudsplitter and I like to get up early and get a walk in before breakfast. The first morning we walked to our Uncle Bill's house. He had passed away the previous May, but through the years, when we came to visit, we had always stayed with him. He left his house to his daughter, our cousin, but we still had a key. We went inside to get nostalgic and have a good cry. We sure do miss him, and always will.

Runningbehind had brought heart shaped cutouts (of the hiking names) from the tee shirts of Maurene and Doris (Womanwithspirit and Dustcatcher). She placed them in a little gauzy see through pouch. We took them on all our hikes so they could be with us. This was a particularly tough hiking trip for Runningbehind as she had recently lost her sister,

Womanwithspirit, who always loved to follow her adventures, and was one of the original hikers.

Meanwhile, back at the ranch, our supper conversation turned to Viagra (Good thing we had the corner table). We discussed having Viagra for women. Blueridgebelle said, "Well, that sounds like a mind-altering drug."

My response to that was, "Yes, it might make you want to have sex when you didn't." Well....

Dinner conversation was always interesting and thought provoking. Our foibles came up often. In true confession style, I told the girls my mother always bought extra large underwear for me (I am a size 6).

Blueridgebelle's sister told her that her nose was too large. These things somehow stick with you all your life. Now I can somewhat understand anorexia.

After supper we would sit on the porch in the many colorful rocking chairs and enjoy the lovely view of the lake. The evenings ended with foot or shoulder massages and more good conversation in the living room area in our annex. And the eternal question: what are we going to do tomorrow?

Winslow State Park is a place that Cloudsplitter and I had driven to with our Uncle Bill for picnics. It is located on the slopes of Mt. Kearsarge, 2,937 feet. We had climbed to the top several years before, and that was our mountain choice that day. It was very wet and slippery on the trail, but once on the top it was bare rock with gorgeous views. We ate our lunches enjoying the scenery.

On the way down, we came to an outcropping where some young girls were doing cute poses on the crest of a large boulder. No one could deny the beautiful background. *Hmmm?* When they left, we took their places. We all took a try with varying degrees of success in the cuteness department, but with those props, no one could get a bad picture. We looked like conquerors!

We went to the New London Barn Playhouse, the oldest continuously operating summer theatre in New Hampshire. It is on the state's register of historical places, and has been in operation since 1933. The evening's performance was the musical *Forever Plaid*.

We got our tickets that afternoon and our seats were in the balcony, first and second row. We were just about head level with the actors and it was a wonderful performance with great seats. The talented lads entertained.

The next day after breakfast, (after we picked up our lunches), we headed to Mt. Ascutney in Vermont. This was another mountain that I had never climbed. Blueridgebelle, Runningbehind and Thunderfoot dropped Cloudsplitter and I off at the Futures Trail while they drove to the parking lot a mile from the summit. By the time we made it to the top they had eaten their lunch, so we all went to the West Peak Vista Overlook.

This overlook is considered one of the premier hang gliding sites in New England. There is a nice wooden platform for takeoff. It made an excellent lunch and relaxing spot for us as no one was there hang gliding.

Near the very top was an observation tower 24.5 feet tall which has plaques identifying the mountains in the 360 degree view. The tower was constructed from sections of an old fire tower which was used until 1952. Unfortunately, the true summit of Ascutney, 3,144 feet, is graced with cell phone towers which drastically ruins the ambience of the summit and is a sad indication of today's world.

After our lunch we hiked down and drove to Cornish, New Hampshire, to see the Cornish-Windsor Bridge which is an old covered bridge 460 feet long that connects New Hampshire to Vermont. The Connecticut River flows under it. It had recently been refurbished. This awesome bridge is the longest covered bridge in the United States and the longest two span wooden bridge in the world. There is a gorgeous view of Mt. Ascutney and the river below making it is a popular photo stop.

We had just enough time for a quick stop at Saint-Gauden National Historical Park in Cornish. This was the residence of Augustus Saint-Gauden who was America's foremost sculptor. His home was also the center of the Cornish Art Colony.

We arrived just as the ranger was cashing out. He said we could go see the grounds and the building until they closed in 15 minutes. The weather was spectacular and there was a great view of Mt. Ascutney from the gracious home's porch. We took a quick look at the gardens and sculptures. The art work was awe inspiring and humbling and of course, the entrance price was just right.

We made it back to Twin Lake Village in time for supper.

Yeah! Once again, we were being fussed over by our waitress, sub-waitress and jelly girl.

We were all incredulous about our many choices and were in complete agreement about how lucky we were to be waited on hand and foot. It was great! Blueridgebelle leaned in to the table and lowered her voice and said, "Now I know how men feel."

The next day we decided to take advantage of all the wonderful facilities that Twin Lake Village had to offer. After breakfast we played tennis, Thunderfoot and Cloudsplitter vs. Runningbehind and I. It was a close match, but Runningbehind and I won.

Thunderfoot and Cloudsplitter tried to blame it on a very low flying airplane and the fact that Runningbehind and I had brought our own tennis rackets. They had to play with TLV's very used wooden rackets, etc. Well, you get the picture.

We took our lunches up the trail to the Ledges, an overlook behind the hotel. There was a great view of Little Sunapee Mountain and the surrounding area. When we got back Thunderfoot and Cloudsplitter played some golf and we all went to the lake and did varying degrees of getting wet. Blueridgebelle was the only one that went swimming, but the rest of us had wet ankles.

The following day it was rainy, so we didn't do any hikes. We did rainy day chores (laundry and shopping) and headed to the Telephone Museum in Warner. Thunderfoot was especially interested in going as her father worked for the phone company.

Even though Cloudsplitter's father-in-law and brother-in-law worked for the phone company, she thought it would be a little boring. As it turned out, it was extremely interesting, and we all enjoyed it.

Next stop was at Mt. Kearsarge Indian Museum. We arrived a half hour before closing, but paid the entrance fee and did a bum's rush tour. Again, it was more interesting than we first thought and along with the museum, there was a Medicine Woods which had paths through the forest with labeled plants and their medicinal properties. I got my picture taken in a semi-real teepee, I was in my element.

One night after supper, we briefly ran into an older man who said to Thunderfoot, "Wow, you are showing them all over." No one quite understood what he meant, and didn't give it much thought.

After sitting on the porch, we headed toward the annex and up the stairs. The same man came out of an extra bathroom on our floor. He said, "Oh, you are showing them suite #2?" and started following Thunderfoot down the hall. The rest of us were telling him that it was our suite, so he finally gave up and went back downstairs.

We were all disturbed by him as he was acting so weird. Thunderfoot was specifically creeped out about it as TLV is a "no locks" establishment. Thunderfoot and I went down to advise the owners.

On the way, we ran into him again and I asked him a few questions to try to draw information out of him and then went to the front desk. We were told he had been a guest there for over 30 years. The lady said that he probably enjoyed his cocktail party too much. Nevertheless, we were still uneasy and solved the situation by placing two chairs and a table in front of our door. At least, we would hear an intruder falling among the furniture.

Later that night Blueridgebelle teased Thunderfoot about having a sign on her back saying, "Talk to me or approach me." We all laughed but Thunderfoot, who had the closest bedroom to the unlocked door. She had a very uneasy night's sleep. Next day, we broke the rules and bought a hook and eye for the door. Thunderfoot slept much better that night.

The dance hall was used several times during the week in the evening. There was bingo, children's programs and dancing. We would watch from the stairs. On those nights, we would go to bed with the sound of music and laughter drifting up from below. (Where are you Patrick?)

Our last hike was up Mount Sunapee—2,726 feet. It is a well-known ski area in southern New Hampshire. I had skied there many times in years past and my Uncle Bill certainly had too. In New Hampshire, you ski for free once you are 70 years old. My uncle was in the ski troops during WWII and was an avid skier. He loved the four letter "F" word ("Free!"), so I guess I come by it naturally, too.

From the ski area parking lot, we chose to go up the Monadnock-Sunapee Trail. The complete trail is 50 miles long and runs between the two mountains. My sister had attempted to do this with a friend many years before. Unfortunately, her friend was ill equipped and by the time they made it to the top of Mt. Sunapee, which was the first four miles, her friend had drunk all her water and was severely dehydrated. They managed to make it back down the mountain, but it was a scary lesson for them both.

There is a ski lodge on the top of Sunapee. It was closed for summer, but we ate lunch and relaxed on the decks. The view, of course, was spectacular and Runningbehind meandered off by herself to gaze at the beauty. I could see her standing by herself looking at the mountains. I couldn't help thinking that it was in a contemplative way, perhaps reflecting on her dear sister's passing. I left her alone.

Later, Runningbehind shared with us what happened while she was staring so intently into the sky.

"While standing on the porch of the lodge overlooking the valley, I noticed something coming very fast from my left. I looked up expecting to see a large bird, but to my astonishment the sky was brilliantly aglow, filled with rainbow shaded clouds, and in the midst of the clouds was my sister, Maurene.

"I saw only her face. She wasn't young and she wasn't old. She was heavenly. Maurene's joyous smile held me spell bound. Time was suspended as I basked in her radiant smile.

Suddenly, Maurene began to move across the sky. I followed along the porch as far as I could. Just as she slipped into the blue of the sky, I heard her laugh. Maurene's laughter resounded with absolute, pure joy and then, I cried."

The last morning came way too quickly and we paid our cash only gratuities to our attentive wait staff. Boy, were we going to miss those sweet young ladies.

Blueridgebelle left first in her rental for her early morning flight. I took everyone else and their luggage in my tiny Corolla to the Manchester Airport late morning. Thunderfoot asked me if I minded if she left her hiking boots in the car. Of course, I didn't, but I hadn't realized that I would have those old boots in my trunk until I went back to Florida in late October. (Actually, I kind of miss them.)

Twin Lake Village is the kind of place that makes you feel like it is your own special vacation spot. I could easily go there every year. We all loved it!

Chapter 16

Grand Teton National Park, Wyoming —2016

Wind River Range, Wyoming

Laurie Chandley, AKA Blueridgebelle

During last year's New Hampshire trip, we had a conversation with a lady who had hiked all over the world. She said her favorite hike in the United States was the Wind River Range in Wyoming. We googled it and the pictures were incredible. We all agreed we had to hike there. The next summer the Happy

Hikers booked flights to Jackson Hole, the closest airport to Pinedale, a small town in the Wind River Range.

My preparation for this hike did not go well. Six weeks before the trip, I was hiking at the North Carolina Arboretum. About a mile and a half into the hike, I stepped on a stone and it rolled over turning my left ankle.

This was not just a little rollover, but one where I could actually feel the ground with my ankle bone. The ankle swelled to the size of a grapefruit. I was black and blue from my toes to my mid-calf. I used ice to stop the swelling and elevated my leg for three weeks. At the end of the three weeks, I began walking again. Then I added strengthening exercises. It was going to be a challenge to do strenuous hiking in Wyoming.

A week before the trip my husband found a triple support ankle brace online. It was an amazing find. Basketball players use them when injured, so he figured it could help me. Without that brace I would have been unable to do most of the hikes.

We were all booked for travel on Delta airline. The Sunday before our Tuesday departure the airline lost access to all of its logistics programs. There was no communication with pilots, map systems, ticketing, baggage and security. Flights were canceled all over the country.

On Monday, we were all communicating about our flight status. I was the driver and had booked the rental car, so I needed to be there to pick up everyone as they arrived. By Monday night the airline had some of their systems running. They were scrambling to match their logistics system with the location of their stranded planes.

Runningbehind was flying from Orlando and would meet me in Charlotte. It was a happy moment when she came off that plane. From Charlotte we traveled through Chicago to Jackson Hole with only short delays.

Throughout the day we received updates from Cloudsplitter and Thunderfoot who were departing from Ft. Myers, Florida. They were rebooked to try again the next day. Through them, we learned that Runswithdogs had made it to Salt Lake City, Utah, but missed her connection to Jackson Hole.

Runningbehind and I picked up the rental car just as darkness fell. We found the Virginian Hotel without much problem. The desk clerk allowed us to check in even though the reservation was in Cloudsplitter's name.

We were all booked together in one room. What a treat! It would be one big slumber party. After dinner, we learned that Runswithdogs was stuck in Salt Lake City and would not arrive until the next day. Runswithdogs would end up sleeping on the floor in the Salt Lake City airport.

We awoke to a beautiful sunny day. During breakfast, we looked over brochure maps of the Teton area. We were afraid to go too far until we knew when the others would arrive. We decided to take a walk around Jackson Hole. We saw the ski resorts, the rodeo grounds and an area of beautiful cottages where locals lived.

The yards were all planted with flowers as if a flower garden competition was in progress. During the walk, we were informed that Runswithdogs would arrive just after noon. Cloudsplitter and Thunderfoot would arrive late afternoon if all went well.

I told Runningbehind we had time to drive the outer portion of the Teton Loop through the valley floor. Once we picked up the others, we would take the inner portion of the loop. The valley floor included the National Elk Refuge. We looked for elk and bison during the drive but did not see any. The Teton Mountains appeared as a backdrop to the valley below. They rose straight from the ground and their majestic presence took our breath away.

We picked up Runswithdogs just after noon and took some time inside the airport to admire a beautiful copper topography mural of the Snake River and the Teton area. Outside there were unique sculptures of western scenes. One especially stunning sculpture was of a cowboy breaking a horse. It was created in 2016 and called "Battle of Wills." These were things we had missed coming into the airport late the night before.

I drove to a cafe on the Teton Loop, so that Runswithdogs could get a good meal. Airport food does not offer her much as she is a vegetarian. We took our food to the top porch. The view from that open air porch of the Teton Range was stunning. A wonderful treat for Runswithdogs after being cooped up in an airport and airplane for over 24 hours.

We walked around the area to let Runswithdogs stretch her legs for a bit. During the walk we determined that since Yellowstone was so close, we would drive at least to the park sign and a few overlooks. That way we would not have already driven the entire Teton Loop without Thunderfoot and Cloudsplitter.

Visiting Yellowstone National Park was not in our original plans for this trip, but it is always fun to take our picture at a park entrance sign. How could we be this close and not do so?

There were many incredible places to stop for views on the north side of the Tetons. At the Oxbow Bend Turnout there were many visible glaciers. The Snake River wound around the Tetons and the lake reflected them. Many Indian tribes lived in this area during warm months. They would all relocate south during the harsh winter months. These were views we would have missed had we stayed on the Jackson Hole side of the Tetons.

When we got to the sign it offered a view of the Snake River and surrounding valley. Signs indicated that the Teton fault is like a large hinge with the Teton Mountains on one side and the Yellowstone Valley on the other. Earthquakes have occurred and occasionally still do.

We took pictures, but no one else was there to take our group picture. Runswithdogs noticed two handsome motorcycles pull up and park. The guys riding them were not bad either. I offered to take their picture if they would take ours. They were happy to do that!

We decided to ride into the park to be able to say we had been there. After all, we can't have entrance sign pictures without actually going inside. At the entrance guard gate we learned there was a fire in the valley and traffic was backed up further in. After driving about a mile into the park I turned around. We could not afford to get trapped in traffic and be late to the airport. We stopped at a small store back in the Tetons to get a drink. I found Yellowstone pins and got one for each of us.

We arrived back at the airport just in time to meet Cloudsplitter and Thunderfoot. There was time to drive the Teton Mountain Range side of the Loop. We made a number of overlook stops that meandered along the Snake River. One of the most spectacular was the overlook where Ansel Adams took his famous photograph of the river with the Teton Range as the backdrop.

Another memorable stop was at the Chapel of the Sacred Heart. Cloudsplitter, and the rest of us, really like to visit churches. It was a rustic log chapel built in 1937, beautifully maintained by the Park Service, and Sunday services are still held there today.

At least Cloudsplitter and Thunderfoot had not lost their entire day. They also gained a nice airline comp for a future trip. It was fun rooming all together again. That does not happen very often with the five of us, but the room had three queen beds. That evening was spent catching up with everyone. It was a great slumber party.

The next morning Cloudsplitter and Runswithdogs were up early, as usual, for coffee and a walk. They hiked a trail that led up the mountain behind the Virginian. After breakfast, we headed to the Craig Thomas Discovery and Visitor Center to get more detailed maps of the area and let Thunderfoot talk to a park ranger.

The rangers indicated that bears were pretty familiar with

people and knew backpacks held food. If confronted we should drop the backpack and back away slowly. The purchase of bear spray was encouraged. We purchased one.

The visitor center had information about the park's animals and ecosystem. There was a large bear statue, along with displays of animals and birds that lived in the park. A large topography map showed the magnitude of the Teton Range. The center had information on the National Elk Refuge in the valley between the Tetons and Jackson Hole. Many elk, especially those disabled or with young, wintered in the refuge instead of moving southeast through the animal migration corridor.

Our first hike was to Inspiration Point. It began with a short flat hike to Jenny Lake. From there, we took a ferry across the lake to a landing point at the trailhead. There were two portions to this hike. The second continued past Inspiration Point over the mountain pass. Cloudsplitter and Runswithdogs took off planning to do both sections.

Thunderfoot, Runningbehind and I set off at a more leisurely pace. I was actually very glad that Runswithdogs had joined the group. I no longer had to push myself so hard to keep up with Cloudsplitter. I could enjoy nature and the scenery now. My focus shifted to taking pictures of the mosses and flora that grew along the trail. I could even linger and let Thunderfoot and Runningbehind go ahead, only pushing to catch up from time to time.

The trail wound back and forth across the mountain face until it flattened out along creeks and waterfalls that fed the lake and Snake River. Many rustic bridges had been built to make this hike possible. These creeks were so cold I could not soak my feet to reduce my ankle swelling.

Once through that area of rushing creeks, a climb began again to the overlook. The viewpoint stood at 7,200 feet. The view was amazing of the lake, valley and western mountain ranges in the distance. We sat for over an hour, had lunch and enjoyed the view.

When Cloudsplitter and Runswithdogs returned to Inspiration Point they had quite a story to tell. They were hiking behind a woman and her two daughters. All of a sudden a large bear ambled out of the woods and crossed the trail just in front of the girls—no warning and no noise.

The bear swung its head around and looked at them. It was very startling. Everyone froze and quit breathing. Then the bear continued back into the woods as if on a mission. No backpacks had to be abandoned. We hated we missed that wildlife experience, but had enjoyed our respite at the point. We took our time hiking down to the ferry and made many stops along the way to enjoy the waterfalls.

The next morning, we packed and drove to Pinedale to see the Wind River Range. The drive was impressive. There were many wide open spaces, ranches, horses and longhorns along the way. Thunderfoot had read that a large wildfire had closed the main highway the week before.

For the first time I really understood how devastating fire could be to the area. An entire mountain range had been burned when the fire jumped the highway. Thankfully, it had been contained so that this part of the trip could still be completed. It made me wonder what the fire in Yellowstone had done a couple of days before.

We checked into our Pinedale hotel by late afternoon. It was one of only three in the town. Then we went to explore downtown Pinedale. There were colorful flower baskets hung from quaint light poles. The visitor center wasn't open, so we stopped at the local outfitters. I purchased a new backpack from the Great Outdoor Shop as a strap had broken on my old one.

One gentleman working there was a wealth of information. Thunderfoot talked to him about the area and hiking options.

We discovered this area was really a backpacking, fishing and hunting destination. There were not many day hiking opportunities but some were identified. We believed it would be enough to keep us occupied during our three day stay. He recommended dinner at the Stockman Restaurant. We enjoyed our meal there and talked to locals about the area.

The next morning Cloudsplitter and Runswithdogs came back from their early coffee run with another incredible story. This time on their walk, they came across a moose and its calf walking down the main street of Pinedale. Unbelievable! Not fair! They were getting to see all the wildlife on this trip. It was still not enough to get Thunderfoot, Runningbehind and me out of bed early the next morning to join them.

Before getting to the trailhead for the day's hike, we stopped at a vista of the vast Wind River Mountain Range. A large engraved plaque there visually identified over 12 named mountains we could see from that vantage point. It gave us a small idea of what we were going to see. The mountain peaks were in the 10,000–13,000 foot range. The view of the range was even more dramatic as we got closer.

A bit further up the road we found the parking area. We gathered our things and headed up an old gravel road. There were many varieties of wildflowers in full bloom. The hike that day did not actually have a trail name. The only marking for our trail was supposed to be a rock cairn and we hoped that it had not been destroyed.

Deep in the valley was an exclusive lodge. It had a helicopter pad for its guests. Other visitors hike into the valley then hike out. Supplies are ferried by llamas.

We soon met a group of llamas and hikers coming down the trail. We stopped to admire the llamas. Many of the hikers were fisherman who had spent time fishing in the rivers and lakes. They said the lodge was beautiful.

Further in, Thunderfoot spotted the rock cairn that marked the turnoff to the trail we wanted to take. The trail wound up and down through alpine meadows for miles. There were so many pine trees down all over the mountain. Sometimes it looked like tumbled Lincoln Logs. In the midst of that tree destruction, all types of wildflowers were blooming.

As the trail began to climb the terrain turned rocky. We passed into a boulder field that opened to the incredible view at the edge of the cliffs. This is what we had come to see. The panoramic view seemed too majestic to be real.

Our pictures looked like we were sitting in front of a painted backdrop. Two lakes were far below in the valley gorge. Long Lake spreads out toward the right with the lodge at the far end. Freemont Lake spreads out to the left.

One of the girls noticed two young men sitting on a rock outcropping with their legs swinging over the edge. I was not sure if they were brave or not too bright. All I could imagine was what would happen if that rock gave way. We sat enjoying some quiet time and our lunch at the point. I have never felt so small or closer to nature than in this location.

There were only two restaurants in town. We thought we would try the local craft brewery and tavern for dinner that night. The parking lot was full and the place was packed. When we learned the wait time, we made a decision to go back to the Stockman Restaurant. The food and service was good for a reasonable price. From then on we ate dinner there every night. We got to know our waitress and talked about our hikes each evening.

After dinner, we walked around a small city park that was part of the Yellowstone Wildlife Corridor. Per a plaque in the park the corridor "protects the longest terrestrial mammal migration in North America." We were hoping to see some wildlife as it was close to dusk, but no such luck. It was still a wonderful way to spend the evening.

The next day we hiked in the Bridger National Forest. There we found a trail into the Green River Lakes area. It was a beautiful valley with a large lake surrounded by mountains. At the end of the lake was a mountain formation that reminded me of Devils Tower National Monument which is also in Wyoming. Huge boulders, the size of large houses, looked like they had been tumbled down the mountain sides. We took the Lakeside Trail.

As we started out, a group of handsome cowboys watered their horses in the lake and then went down the trail in front of us. Thunderfoot, Runningbehind and I went at an easy pace. This would be the longest hike I had taken since turning my ankle. It would be a true test of the brace I had been wearing.

There were fishermen on the lake completing the tranquil views. At the end of the lake the trail turned left into a slot canyon, and we viewed a multitiered waterfall that fed the lake. The trail wound into a high valley with meadow grasslands, creeks and small lakes. White birches dotted the landscape everywhere in the valley.

Cloudsplitter and Runswithdogs hiked ahead to see a stone natural bridge. My ankle had started to swell and I was feeling some discomfort. I told Thunderfoot and Runningbehind that I needed to turn around and head back. They both wanted to see the bridge and did not want me to stop because there was only one bear spray. I told them I would leave it with them. I would be fine going back to the car on my own, but they were uncomfortable with that. So I continued the best I could. When Cloudsplitter and Runswithdogs came back, they told us that the bridge was interesting, but still quite a long hike.

We all turned around to head back to the car. By this point, I was a little concerned about my ability to hike out. We made it to the lake and sat down to take a break. Resting turned out to be a very bad idea for me. My ankle was actually swelling more after the rest.

We traveled down the lakeside slowly. About half way down the lake Thunderfoot and Runningbehind wanted to take another break. I told them if I sat down I was not going to get back up again. I headed off without them making a beeline for the car. My ankle was painful and swelling. I had overdone it.

I waved hello to Cloudsplitter and Runswithdogs as I passed them by the lake's edge. Once I made it to the car I knew I had pushed it too far. I hoped one rest day would be enough to settle it down. If not, then the hikes I had been able to do had been incredible enough.

The next day the others did another lakeside hike at Half Moon Lake. En route to the trailhead, I passed a restaurant with small rental cabins up on the mountainside. There were a few cars and some men in the parking lot. We stopped to see if this was a place I could wait for them. It was perfect.

In the back was a porch with tables that overlooked the lake and a small marina. It was closed, but I thought that no one would be upset if I used it to read and have lunch. I dropped the girls at the trailhead then drove back to the restaurant.

Once I was settled at a table, I read for awhile then opened my lunch. I heard voices on the other side of the wall from where I was sitting. Looking through a window, the men I had seen earlier were sitting at the bar having drinks. I wondered if I could buy a cold beer or soft drink to go with my lunch.

I walked to the front of the building and found a door that led directly to the bar. A man behind the bar was serving Moscow Mules. I asked if I could buy a beer. The man said the register was closed and offered me a Moscow Mule. At the time I did not even know what that drink was so declined.

The man asked what beer I wanted and opened one passing it over the bar to me. I offered him money and he refused. I didn't want him to get in trouble. Turned out he was the owner of the restaurant and cabins.

We chatted for awhile. They asked where I was from and what I was doing there. I explained our group and how we had ended up in Pinedale. They all found it very interesting that word about their area and small town was getting out into the hiking community.

They had been fishing that morning and were having a drink together before heading home. I thanked them profusely for letting me interrupt and told them I wished the restaurant was open that night. I enjoyed my cold beer, and lunch with a view.

After I had eaten, the restaurant manager came out and asked if I would like another beer. I declined, but asked if I could use the restroom. I had a nice talk about the area with him and his wife, who cooked for the restaurant. The rest of the time was spent reading. It was a lovely afternoon.

Thunderfoot was the first to join me lakeside. She was

surprised to see the beer sitting there. I told everyone about my adventure. The girls talked to the manager as well and took a look around. We told him if we ever came back we would be sure to eat there. We hated that they were not open that day, because it was our last evening in Pinedale. They let us know about a wonderful area to take sunset pictures, which we did, later that evening.

We found time that afternoon to tour the Mountain Man Museum. It was very small, but contained a lot of interesting antique artifacts from local families. Most items were related to the pioneering and trapping lifestyle. We had our last meal in Pinedale at the Stockman Restaurant.

We took off early the next morning and returned to Jackson Hole. Our last hike in Wyoming was to Taggert Lake. We hiked past some mule stables and entered into an almost desert type environment.

The trail was fairly flat and wound around grassland meadows with a backdrop of the Teton Mountain Range. The trail ended at an emerald green lake. The Tetons seemed to drop straight down on the opposite shore. We found rocks to sit on and enjoyed the calming beauty with our lunch. A friendly man took a group picture of us, all in pink, perched on a large rock. It is still one of my favorites.

After the hike, we went to the National Museum of Wildlife Art. This museum has some of the most realistic animal sculptures and art works I had ever seen. The sculptures are both inside and outside. The building itself is made from red sandstone and was modeled after the Slains Castle in Scotland. We found a room completely dedicated to the historic posters from each of the National Parks. As Thunderfoot, Cloudsplitter, and Runningbehind went through the room, they found only two parks they had not seen.

From there we went to the historic Jackson Hole town square. We caught sight of two stagecoaches and the Jackson Hole Antler Arch Park in the center of town. These arches are at the four corners of the park. Each was built with a steel frame and authentic elk antlers.

After dinner I asked to stop by the Million Dollar Cowboy Bar. I had seen it in movies and wanted to at least sit on the iconic saddle barstools. It wasn't open yet, but after a request to the bouncer, we were let in for a quick visit and a beer at the bar.

We spent one more slumber party night at the Virginian before flying home the next morning. In terms of the trips I have made with the Happy Hikers, this was one of the best. My heartfelt thanks go out to the lady that recommended hiking in the Wind River Range. It is definitely one I would love to revisit.

Chapter Seventeen

Cape Breton Island, Nova Scotia
Cape Breton Highlands National Park, Nova Scotia
—2017

Victoria Park, Truro, Nova Scotia

Cleo Simon, AKA Runningbehind

July thirtieth was our day to travel that year. Our destination was Halifax, Nova Scotia. I was lucky to get a direct flight from Orlando, Florida, and had an easy late afternoon travel time.

Cloudsplitter and Thunderfoot left from Ft. Myers, Florida. Cloudsplitter breezed through the pre-check line with Thunderfoot right behind her. Security couldn't get Thunderfoot's ticket to scan. Cloudsplitter, free and clear, (on the other side) watched in puzzlement while Thunderfoot had to leave pre-check and was sent back to the regular checkout line.

There she had to remove her shoes, belt, jacket, backpack, and liquids that were in her bag. Next, she went under the wand. The security guard did more checking online and finally her ticket was cleared and she was allowed to go through.

Walking up to Cloudsplitter a little frazzled, but relieved, Thunderfoot teasingly said, "What trick were you playing on me?" Cloudsplitter had purchased and printed both boarding passes, but somehow only Thunderfoot's ticket had been defective!

Thunderfoot and Cloudsplitter were the first to arrive at 7:30 p.m. in Halifax. Blueridgebelle and I flew in two hours later. We had an excited welcome all around. We then went to the hotel and would return at twelve midnight for the late arrival of Runswithdogs.

We watched in anticipation as we waited by the gate at midnight, but no Runswithdogs appeared. The airport was deserted by now so Cloudsplitter tried to find out what had happened and someone finally told her to check the 2:00 a.m. flight. We were frantically waiting when she suddenly appeared at the top of the stairs. Runswithdogs made a grand entrance and four Happy Hikers cheered. She immediately told us that her connecting flight had been delayed.

We didn't make it to bed until after 3:00 a.m. We slept in and had a later start to our first day in Nova Scotia than planned. Our destination was Cape Breton Island to hike in the national park. We headed east on route 104 eager to explore. It would take us five hours to get to the park, but we had a lot of catching up to do, and scenery to watch.

We stopped for lunch outside of Inverness. We always wear our matching Happy Hiker shirts, a different color for each day. People often stop us and ask about them. We meet so many interesting people that way and get good advice about trails from fellow hikers. Our shirts also have our trail names, so that makes for added conversation.

At the restaurant, a gentleman came to our table and asked where we planned to hike. He told us about a trail in Mabou. We knew it had to be good coming from a local. He then told us the Skyline Trail, our destination, was for tourists.

When we reached downtown Inverness, a city on the west coast of Cape Breton Island, we stopped at the Visitor Center to get maps and information about trails in the area. We did pick up a Mabou map and that trail sounded like it would be perfect for us.

At the Visitor Center, we were directed to a boardwalk that goes from the town down to the ocean. It was a gorgeous day and the walk was just what we needed after being in the car for so long. On the north side of the boardwalk was the Cabot Links Golf Course. They were playing a serious tournament as all the caddies had their player's name on the back of their shirts. It looked very official.

The course ran along the beach. I don't know how the players stayed focused with such a beautiful view.

We walked the beach looking for shells and colorful stones. Cloudsplitter saves heart shaped rocks and that day she found a perfect one. The ocean is always intriguing and was much enjoyed amid the comradeship of friends.

Our last stop for the day was Cheticamp where we would be staying at the Cornerstone Motel. Cheticamp is a colorful fishing village on the Cabot Trail that overlooks a scenic harbor. A large portion of the residents are Acadians and speak French. Cheticamp is at the entrance to the Cape Breton Highland National Park, our hiking destination.

Day two we were up early eager to hike the Skyline Trail. We went to Evangeline's for breakfast. It quickly became a favorite. They had friendly staff, good food and a great view of the harbor. We always had stimulating conversations there. That morning it was "spam, spare parts with ham." Our parents all served it, we all ate it, but when we analyzed it, our collective opinion was "gross!"

After leaving Evangeline's, we headed north on the Cabot Trail. That trail was 185 miles in length and loops around the northern part of Cape Breton Island. The area was often called the Celtic heart of North America. Since Blueridgebelle, Cloudsplitter's husband and I have Scottish ancestry, we were excited to be there and sampled as much Scottish culture as we could.

Our car wound along the edge of Mt. French on the way to the trailhead. Off to the left at the headland cliff, we were able to see hikers at the top of the Skyline Trail. From that distance, the hikers looked like tiny dots. The Cabot Trail continued to wind through green mountains on one side and offered ocean vistas on the other. The cliffs were rugged and jagged as they reached down to touch the sea.

Destination reached, we gathered our backpacks, water, and for me, my walking stick, and started our hike. The Skyline Trail began as a walk through the woods. About halfway, we reached a boardwalk which led us to the top. The trail was a five mile loop with a 1,330 foot elevation gain. At the top we could see forever. The ocean was before us, with its rugged coast line, and down below we could see the Cabot Trail that brought us here.

Our goal is always to have lunch with a view and we were enthralled with this one. We walked the boardwalk along the top just as the hikers we had seen earlier. Now, we were the moving dots at the top of the mountain. We all sat eating our lunches, totally blissful, trying to store away the moment. Even though the trail was busy with lots of tourists, we loved being there.

We probably spent two or three hours at the top and then ambled back down the trail. Cloudsplitter and Runswithdogs chose to do the longer route and they were gifted with seeing a moose and her calf on that trail. It pays to go the extra mile!

Back at the trailhead, there was a line of much needed

portajohns. Thunderfoot grabbed the door of one that said vacant and swung it open. To her shock she provided a public viewing of a man who had neglected to lock the door. She slammed the door, and was so embarrassed that the teasing and many quips were saved for dinner's entertainment. We did Thunderfoot justice!

That night, we dined at a pub that had a wonderful fiddler by the name of McDougle. Toe tapping was mandatory. Toward the end of the evening a local man did some lively Celtic dancing to entertain the crowd. We responded with enthusiastic clapping and by shouting words of encouragement.

Next day, we were up early and off to breakfast. First though, we had to stop and get gasoline which Blueridgebelle had done every morning. Unfortunately, we had rented a real gas guzzler. We then went to Evangeline's in Cheticamp for breakfast. Every trip we take we have opportunities to poke fun at one another. As we get older we seem to relish silly moments more and more. For this trip my favorite "pick" happened on that particular morning.

Runswithdogs had a sore on the side of her nose. Without our knowing, Cloudsplitter told her that honey may help. So Runswithdogs took a packet of honey from the table, opened it, and put the honey on her finger. She then slid it along the side of her nose and licked her finger.

Now to Blueridgebelle sitting at the other end of the table at an angle, it looked as though Runswithdogs had picked her nose and then licked her finger. Blueridgebelle began to laugh hysterically and of course with such a belly laugh going on Thunderfoot and I began to laugh also, and wanted to know what happened.

Blueridgebelle finally calmed down and told us what she saw. She thought Runswithdogs was trying to be funny. When all was explained, we laughed until we were weak. Naturally, we accused Cloudsplitter of playing a trick on her sister. Whoever heard of putting honey on a sore? Cloudsplitter did inform us later that honey really is an old remedy for sores. I recently read an article in a magazine stating the same—live and learn.

Leaving the restaurant in great spirits, we went to Cheticamp Island for a hike along the cliffs. The island was like a prairie with a grove of pine trees near the top. We saw numerous ocean birds and one very majestic bald eagle.

Near the cliffs, I met two very well dressed men. I told them if I had known this was a "black tie" trail I would have dressed more appropriately. They laughed and were very friendly, but never did explain their attire. There were some lots for sale on the island and I speculated that might be the reason they were there.

We next traveled to Mabou to follow the tip from the hiker we met at the restaurant on our way to Cape Breton Island. We hiked the Fair Alistair's Trail. It was a lovely walk through the woods to the cliffs at the top. We devoured the view of the ocean, the shore line, and those wonderful rugged cliffs. This was another lunch with a view! Peanut Butter sandwiches and an apple tasted like "home cooking" with the sight before us.

This was our time to reflect and just let nature bring its joy.

Cloudsplitter and Runswithdogs took a side trail back, the McPhee. They picked a "shirt" full of raspberries and shared them. Again, that extra mile gifted them and this time us, too.

After the hike, we went to charming downtown Mabou. There we found our trip's favorite dinner restaurant. The "Red Shoe Pub" was excellent. The fiddlers were delightful, playing beautiful Celtic music while we dined.

Each morning of the trip, when we always stopped at the gas station, Thunderfoot would ask, "How much gas do we have?"

Blueridgebelle would answer, "A fourth of a tank."

Thunderfoot would then comment, "I don't understand it, we don't go that far."

On this particular day when Blueridgebelle stopped to get gas she started laughing and said, "I don't believe I did this." She had been looking at the temperature gauge all week. It was in the same spot her gas gauge was located in her own car. Nonetheless, she got a lot of ribbing about her "first senior moment." She was the youngest and hadn't yet reached sixty.

After breakfast at Evangeline's, we stopped at the church in Cheticamp. As we went from town to town in Cape Breton we would stop and visit old churches. Each one was very ornate with statues, paintings, and stained glass windows. A few we visited had tartans draped on pillars lining the isles. We assumed that was to designate where each clan would sit. Cloudsplitter had always loved old churches and now we loved them, too.

Back in the car, we traveled north on the Cabot Trail. We

planned to explore the east side of Cape Breton Island.

Our first stop was a scenic overlook to view the Aspy Fault. This fault runs through 40 km of Cape Breton. At the lookout, the sign stated that we were standing halfway down the fault's deep escarpment looking at the Aspy River Valley. It really was quite a sight to look down the valley and to know this was the evidence of the Aspy Fault. Much of the extraordinary scenery in the Cape Breton Highlands was created by Aspy.

Our next stop was the Gampo Abbey, a Western Buddhist monastery. It was located in the Cape Breton Highlands on a cliff overlooking the Gulf of St. Lawrence. It was a very picturesque setting. We walked the trails around the grounds until the abbey opened.

We were guided through the monastery by Gampo's Acharya Ani Pema Chodron. She was born in New York, graduated from Berkeley in California and for many years was an elementary school teacher. In her mid thirties, she began her studies to become a nun. In 1984, she became the first director of Gampo Abbey. When she was giving us a tour of the abbey, we had no idea that she was the principal teacher of the monastery. She told us that she was a "student always learning."

She explained to us that discipline was the core of life at the abbey. Residents had four hours of meditation daily and maintain silence from eight in the evening until noon each day.

We visited the library and its collection of sacred books, and the prayer room full of the monk's cushions. That was where we spent most of our time while she explained life at the abbey.

After our visit with serenity, we were ready for a nature hike. We were told not to miss White Point by the owners of Cornerstone Motel. White Point proved difficult to find. We took various dirt roads and had to back track a few times. Finally, Blueridgebelle turned onto a bumpy dirt road and we knew that had to be the place. The whole scene before us was dotted with white granite rocks.

In the early 1900's, White Point was a bustling community. It had homes, a school, church, lobster processing plant and a saw mill. Now all that was left of the French fishing village were a few stone foundations, a cemetery for the shipwrecked, and a huge cross at the top of the hill marking the final resting place of an unknown soldier.

Many different trails beckoned us to explore this peninsula. White granite rocks abound in the area leading down to the pounding surf. Many of the rugged granite cliffs were a beautiful pink hue. We spent a few hours walking the various paths enjoying the loveliness of that high, grassy plateau. There was just something special about White Point. It reminded us of the moors of Scotland. We all left there having been touched by its simplicity.

Our last stop for the day was Ingonish Ferry. There we stayed at the Knotty Pine Cottages. We all loved the view from the patio overlooking the Ingonish Harbour and the Atlantic Ocean. We ordered take out so we could enjoy the view with our supper. We spent the evening reminiscing, and sipping wine while enjoying the beautiful harbor.

The next morning, while having coffee on the patio overlooking the bay, we discussed our many plans for the day. First on the list was breakfast at the Clucking Chicken. This restaurant had every chicken quote and piece of chicken décor imaginable.

We chose the restaurant because Cloudsplitter has a couple of dozen chickens which she calls "The Ladies." She talks about them with reverence. They are well cared for and loved. In return, they keep her supplied with wonderful fresh eggs and many happy moments.

After breakfast we went to the Gaelic College in St. Anne's. It was founded in 1938, and was the only college of that kind in North America. Its purpose was to promote Gaelic Culture through programs, workshops, and festivals. At the front entrance to the college, we found a bagpiper dressed in Scottish attire.

He was a student at the college and hoped to make his living playing the pipes. He was delightful and played the bagpipes to our heart's content. We did thank him generously.

The gift shop was very interesting. Since Blueridgebelle, Cloudsplitter's husband and I have Scottish ancestors, we all tried to find our tartan. Cloudsplitter got a tartan scarf for her dog and Blueridgebelle and I found a book about the McLains, our ancestors, which included a picture of our tartan. We totally enjoyed our visit at the Gaelic College.

Leaving the college, we followed a tip from a local that suggested we hike Uisge Ban Falls. (Gaelic pronunciation, Ish

Ka Ban Falls.) We also were informed that the area had been greatly damaged by a storm the year before. Even with the storm damage, we had a beautiful hike through the woods to the falls. There we were surprised to be greeted by giant boulders.

The pictures I had seen of Uisge Ban Falls showed a three tiered falls. We only saw the bottom falls gushing into a small pool. It was a lovely area for lunch and for pampering our feet by soaking them in the cold stream. We were disappointed to find the river walk part of the trail was closed, because bridges had been washed away. We had another beautiful hike back through the woods, and left there in high spirits.

This day was definitely one with variety. Next stop was the Alexander Graham Bell Museum in Baddeck. The museum acreage overlooks the Bras d'Or Lake. Across the lake was Bell's summer home still owned by his descendants.

We learned much at the museum. After moving to America from Scotland, Bell set up a school for "Visible Speech" for the deaf. He fell in love with one of his students and married her. Throughout his life he worked to improve the lives of the deaf.

We were amazed to learn that he and his associates achieved Canada's first powered airplane flight and produced the world's fastest boat. Because the telephone so impacted the world, I had been stuck on that one fact.

Probably most amazing to all of us was the fact that he was the author of the term "Greenhouse Effect." In the early 1900's, he warned the world of foreign particles in the air. He stated we had a need for a cleaner energy source to cut down on the world's use of coal and oil. We all left the museum with renewed respect for Alexander Graham Bell.

Cloudsplitter always gets our hotels for us and that evening she directed us to the campus of Francis Xavier University. We all looked at her in puzzlement when we stopped in front of the Governor's Hall. We were all going back to college for a night and staying in the dorm. What great fun it was, and that stay brought back lots of happy memories of dorm life.

Mornings were hectic with five gals and usually only one or two bathrooms to share. After breakfast was always a critical nature time, so we usually headed in different directions to search for "a quiet place."

After racing around the dorm, Cloudsplitter and Blueridgebelle came charging around different corners to a public bathroom. They laughed when they met, did a quick urgency assessment, and then the other one was off searching again.

We finally did get together again that morning. We took our pictures in front of the dorm, and then we were off to the Bay of Fundy. Twice daily, powerful tides race in from the Bay of Fundy to push back the outgoing flow of the Salmon River. We went to the Viewing Center in Truro to witness this.

We chose a spot on some rocks along the river to view the tidal bore. While we were waiting a bus load of young Mennonite ladies arrived and also chose the rocks along the river to sit. They looked like fragile flowers blooming among the rocks with their colorful dresses and little white bonnets. They were lovely to see.

According to the time table, the tidal bore arrived right on time. It was 11:57 a.m. The ripple of the tide was small, but the speed at which it advanced was impressive. It wasn't long before the dry areas of the basin were completely filled with water.

Every six hours, 100 billion tons of sea water rush in and out of the Bay of Fundy producing tides ranging from eleven to fifty-three feet. These are the highest tides in the world. We wanted to be at the Bay of Fundy, but travel time didn't allow us to do that, so we were thankful for the experience we had.

While we were in Truro, we decided to go for our last Nova Scotia hike at Victoria Park. This city park was developed in 1903 due to twenty-five acres being given to the city by a resident. The park had slowly expanded to the current thousand acres.

This amazing park had beautiful trails that go up and down stairs such as Jacob's Ladder with 175 steps. The park had a gorge, river, waterfalls and an old growth hemlock forest.

Cloudsplitter and Runswithdogs raced ahead to do the challenging ladders and trails throughout the park. Jacob's Ladder was first on their list. Thunderfoot, Blueridgebelle and I chose to do a more leisurely trail which led to a beautiful waterfall. We also encountered some of those neat ladders in order to reach the falls. After two hours of delightful hiking through the woods we had to leave and return to Halifax to pack for our return home.

The morning of departure the other girls were up early to catch the airport shuttle for their 6:00 a.m. flight. My flight was at 1:00 p.m. so I slept in, had breakfast, and went to the airport with plenty of time to spare.

Runningbehind was the last Happy Hiker to leave Nova Scotia. During the flight I looked at all the pictures I had taken and relived each day of our wonderful trip. When I landed in Florida, Runningbehind faded into the edges of my mind, and Cleo emerged to happily greet her husband, Ed.

Once home, we gals wash our Happy Hiker T-shirts, and one pink hat. We fold them carefully and store them in a special box where they hibernate for the winter. In the spring, we begin to hear them whisper for they know Blueridgebelle is coming to Florida for a visit.

We will meet up with our other three companions for a reunion in Punta Gorda. We do some hiking in the area and put our heads together to make a list of possible destinations for our summer trip. Research is done and we generally make a decision within a month or two.

This particular visit, the Happy Hikers had an added agenda. Three years ago, we decided to write a book about our hiking adventures. The original plan was to send our memories of each trip to Cloudsplitter, she would compile them and then write the chapter. We would progress chapter by chapter that way.

Three years into that plan we had three chapters done with fourteen to go. Thunderfoot told us, "We need a new plan, or we will run out of life." We went on to plan B. We divided the trips among us and each of us wrote three or four chapters.

By summer our Happy Hiker T-shirts become quite boisterous. They know decisions have been made and a plan is in motion. Excitedly our T-shirts and pink hats are packed into our suitcases. The Happy Hikers are on the move for another fantastic adventure.

We can't wait to reach our chosen destination and eagerly emerge once again as CLOUDSPLITTER, RUNSWITHDOGS, THUNDERFOOT, BLUERIDGEBELLE, and RUNNINGBEHIND.

Epilogue

While finishing this book, we made two more hiking trips. 2018 brought us to New York's wondrous Catskill Mountains where we ended up in a small Ukrainian hamlet. Our accommodations included the very best homemade Ukraine food, freshly prepared each day. (We might just have to keep that spot a secret.)

In 2019 we ventured to the Great Smoky Mountains of North Carolina where we got to spend a night in a wilderness cabin on top of Mount LeConte.

Unfortunately, 2020 was a quiet year for all the hikers due to Covid-19. We curtailed our urges for adventure as best we could and stayed close to home. With such an awesome world out there, it was a very challenging and difficult task.

But, we have great hope for the future. We look forward to new trips and the opportunity to explore many more mountains along our path.

Betsy Campbell

(Cloudsplitter)

My first and foremost belief is that life should be fully entwined with nature. It is too easy to get detached from Mother Nature in today's fast paced electronic world. And as much fun as that can be at times, without nature in my life, I would be like a bird without wings. However, that was a learned belief that evolved through the years.

I was born 13 miles outside of New York City and although that might sound like I didn't have any exposure to the great outdoors, it would be a misconception. My family took evening and weekend walks along the Hutchinson River and in many of New York's beautiful parks. Outdoor picnics, swimming and canoeing were weekend treats and while I was too young to participate in some of these activities, I did get to watch my family enjoy them.

When I was seven years old, I had the very good fortune of having my family move to Temple, New Hampshire. Here was serious country and where my love of nature formulated and grew. Temple was and still is a small, bucolic, New England village in southern New Hampshire surrounded by beautiful mountains with miles and miles of hiking trails. And hike we did. First as a family, then with friends and later just to satisfy the need to get to the top and breathe in the beauty. All mountain tops give me a sense of wellbeing and a connection to what I believe really matters.

Many years later my husband and I moved to Florida with kids, dogs and cats in tow. The mountains were gone, but were replaced with level walks in parks and along country roads. Only summers provided the chance to answer the beckoning of the mountains.

At Rio Paz Tennis Center in Punta Gorda, I met my two friends who would become my future hiking buddies. They also felt the pure pleasure of hiking in the mountains and getting to the top. Together we would choose a new location to explore each year, but always with mountains and hiking as the basis. We were getting our fix. And eventually our new trail names.

My friends were kind enough to let me lead the way and hence, dubbed me forever, Cloudsplitter. It's very hard not to feel a little pride with a handle like that, but it does carry its own amount of responsibility. One does have to know where one is going if they are in the front.

Time rushes on and I am still living in Florida. I definitely prefer temperatures above 60 degrees although I do look forward to the coolness of summers at elevations above 14 feet. My husband and I are fantasizing about retirement while living on a small farm with two pet feral pigs, one dog, four cats and twenty chickens who do not appreciate the heat as much as I do.

As with everyone else, my life is full and hectic except for that one glorious week when several hiking buddies gather together and I can answer the call of the mountains in the company of steadfast friends. And that will do.

Laurie Miller Chandley

(Blueridgebelle)

My parents loved camping and enjoying all of the outdoor adventures offered. We often sang as a family on those long road trips to and from our destination. Both had excellent voices and taught us many of the popular songs from their childhood.

One of my first memories is singing around a campfire. When I looked up, I realized that we were encircled by other campers and their kids who were standing in the dark listening. The next day we played with those kids in the woods and lake. From that moment, I understood how nature brings people together that might not have otherwise met.

Throughout my childhood my family camped and traveled the eastern United States. We spent time in rustic as well as city locations. Our favorite trips were in campgrounds where we could meet people and spend time in the countryside. In my teens and through college I would travel locally in the south with friends to the beach, college sports events and concerts.

As a snow skier, I joined the Charlotte, NC ski club and began ski racing for fun. We traveled to many resorts throughout the east. This changed my focus from camping to hotels and condos. I do like running water and so my camping days were over.

I met my best friend and future husband, Bruce, at a West Virginia ski resort where he was the Marketing Director. We moved to Asheville, NC and were married in 1988. Both of us were very career focused. I was highly motivated and began a career climb that would cover the next 30 years ending as a Director with my company. The loss of young friends and family too early in life changed my perspective on what was important to me. I traveled with a niece who was in college to Italy and this renewed an interest in travel for fun.

In 2007 Bruce had a major medical event and a worse event two years later. His health and life would never be the same. During the two years in between I began hiking and mountain biking in Asheville, NC to reduce stress. This was life changing for me. It also helped Bruce to gain confidence with being on his own while I was out. My activities in the outdoors brought peace and better health.

My mom, Maurene, mentioned that I was hiking to my Aunt Cleo. Shortly after that my phone rang and an invitation was issued. The end result was a relationship with a group of day hikers who my mom had traveled with for annual trips. The group called themselves the Happy Hikers.

I was to pick a trail name. My sister offered up "Blue Ridge Belle." While it did not sound like a native trail name like the others had, I liked the sound of that. My desire to get back into the great outdoors has again introduced me to new friends I would have never met. I am so proud to be hiking with this wonderful group of women. We come each year with ideas for the next year's trip. I look forward to researching and selecting another area of this beautiful country to explore each year.

Nancy Fetzer

(Runswithdogs)

 Growing up in the suburbs of Pelham, New York, I knew I wanted to be in the country. One day I wanted to own and ride a horse, and shoot Indians like they did on television. But it didn't turn out that way.

I did get the horse and found out it was way too much work. I didn't shoot any Indians and as I grew older, I discovered that I didn't want to shoot them, I wanted to be an Indian. They seem to worship the land and the world around them the way the white man doesn't. This was a dilemma for me. Putting the shooting vs. being an Indian issue aside, I got a degree in Physical Education at the University of New Hampshire.

Teaching full time seemed to limit my free time way too much, so I pursued numerous part time jobs most of which I loved. My favorite was waitressing at the Folk Way in Peterborough, NH in the 1980's. The Folk Way was a restaurant with outdoor garden seating and folk music venue in an old Victorian house.

The incredibly talented performers were a pure pleasure to meet and listen to for free, which was one of the perks of the job. Most of the employees were college grads who were looking for something out of the ordinary. And once employed there, they kept their job. Due to the death of the owner, the Folk Way closed, but the employees still get together all these years later and reminisce of their wonderful times there. Collectively,

I think they would all agree that it was more than a job, it was a family working together. To this day, I still travel to hear the same performers only now I have to pay.

When not working my many part time jobs, that freed me up for my more important interests, I pursued my passion of running, tennis and hiking. Team tennis lead me to the nationals twice which was a wonderful honor and the commitment it takes to get there was very gratifying. It also let me see and explore new areas of the country. My team and I played our finals in Tucson, Arizona, and Palm Springs, California, both beautiful places. I also ran many marathons and competed in triathlons with my sister, Cloudsplitter.

With all the same interests as many of the Happy Hikers, one might think that I had been an original member. Unfortunately, I wasn't. In the last eight years of my Dad's life, I lived with him in his home in Florida taking care of him.

Living with Dad at that age does cramp your style, but I still got to squeeze in tennis, hiking and walking. Week long vacations were more difficult, so I just listened to their adventures. The decision to stay with him was, of course, worth it in the end as we enjoyed many fun times that can never be replaced.

So, because of commitments and excuses, I was not able to join the group until 2013. Now I am a member. I think I am a blood sister, sans the blood. (I knew I would get back to my Indian roots.) I enjoy the adventures and camaraderie of the Happy Hikers and can't wait for our next adventure.

Doris Graham

(Dustcatcher)

Doris was born September 20, 1939, on Guam, a small island in the Western Pacific Ocean. She was the oldest of four sisters and one brother. She only made it to four feet eleven inches tall and normally weighed one hundred pounds or less. Doris was little but mighty.

She was the first in her family to travel from Guam to the mainland to attend college, graduating from the College of St. Francis outside of Chicago. This was unheard of for women of her era. She had earlier made a trip to New York and Washington D. C. when she represented Guam as the Cherry Blossom Festival Princess.

After finishing her master's degree, Doris returned home and soon became a member of the "Go Group of Guam," a group of first year teachers from the mainland. With her loving and playful personality she joined the exploring and fun seeking with Cleo and the others.

Doris and Cleo taught on Guam for two years and then took teaching positions in Hawaii where they shared an apartment. Doris met Bill Graham in Hawaii. They married June 17, 1967. With marriage to Bill, Doris was able to continue her adventures.

Doris and Bill lived overseas the last ten years before his retirement. Doris found adventure in abundance. She climbed to the top of Mount Fuji in Japan, ran marathons in front of the Pyramids in Egypt, took a balloon ride over the Masai Mara plains in Kenya, spent one Christmas in the village of Rovaniemi at the North Pole. She took elephant rides around the Taj Mahal in India and Tiger Tops in Nepal, traveled extensively throughout game parks in South Africa and Botswana, went diving off the Barrier Reef in Australia, and walked along the Great Wall of China.

After Bill retired they continued to travel, taking a cruise through the Panama Canal, then to Alaska, Europe and Patagonia. Doris always wanted to explore the Amazon which was in the early stages of planning. Next on their list was a trip in their RV to Alaska.

The last conversation I had with Doris was about a month before she died. We discussed our upcoming trips, Doris and Bill to Alaska and the Happy Hikers to Washington. We promised to call and share our adventures at the end of the summer.

During our conversation, Doris told me about two graduating eighth grade boys who had given her a teddy bear because she was their favorite teacher. She was so thrilled. After retirement, Doris became a substitute teacher. She loved her students and they loved her.

Doris died June 16, 2012, after suffering a brain aneurysm. We will always miss her.

— Compiled by Cleo Simon

Nancy Humphrey

(Thunderfoot)

From my earliest remembrances, comes my love for being outside. It didn't matter how hot or cold it was. I would sit in elementary school watching it snow—itching to get out in it! I lived in what I like to call my "Leave It to Beaver" world; a stay at home mom, a hard working telephone man for a Dad, and four brothers that all went to a neighborhood school and church. We played games, walked to school, played outside until dark, and never were hungry or afraid. It was a childhood I wish all children could have!

One of my childhood friends and I always went out exploring around my hometown, Centralia, Illinois. Sometimes we went to different parts of town and sometimes we would walk out into the country. We liked to climb in the windows of vacant houses. We never broke or hurt anything. We just looked for treasures in the attics or basements. Once we climbed into a house we thought was empty and it wasn't. Boy, oh boy, that sure scared us. We went flying back out the window as fast as we could. I guess walking and exploring were always part of me.

I lived in this simple world until my last two years of college when I moved to Nashville, Tennessee, to go to a church college. While I was in college I played for the volleyball team. What I liked best about that was traveling to all the different schools, especially the schools that were in the mountainous regions of Tennessee and Kentucky. This began my love for being in the mountains. As far as my education during college, I really didn't know what I wanted to be. They put me in the teacher program. I became a teacher and ended up teaching for 35 years in Arcadia, FL.

While teaching at DeSoto Middle School in Arcadia, I became friends with another teacher, Cleo Simon—Runningbehind. She also had a love for exploring nature. Cleo and I would hike, bike, and kayak all the parks, creeks and rivers in the area including a canoe trip down in the Florida Keys. We began to take longer trips together, for instance, we went on a snorkeling trip in the area around Cancun, Mexico. We also went on a fall leaves trip along the Blue Ridge Parkway with her sister, Maurene—Womanwithspirit.

In the summer of 1992 one of our tennis friends, Betsy Campbell—Cloudsplitter invited us to her summer home in New Hampshire. Cleo, Maurene and I decided to go. This was the beginning of our group known as the Happy Hikers. It also started another great adventure with my friend, Betsy, which was hiking the high points of each state. Through highpointing, Betsy and I have hiked and explored every U.S. State but Hawaii.

Sometimes I sit in my recliner in my family room and think about how blessed I am to have a nice home, great family, and adventurous friends known as the Happy Hikers that have taken me to many beautiful places and on so many wonderful adventures. Let the adventures continue!

Maurene Johannsen Miller

(Womanwithspirit)

I was the middle daughter in a farming family in Minnesota. Farming in general does not allow for many vacations or travel. It was a lot of work for the entire family. As a result, a yearning for adventure and travel was always present in my soul. I took my younger sister, Cleo, and her friends on adventures as often as my free time allowed.

I met my husband, Bob, at a local dance. He was my cousin's date, but a connection was made and with her permission we began dating. My first major trip was to California to marry Bob before he shipped out with the Navy to Guam. My parents and I drove cross country to join him and then back home. It was interesting to see the variety of this great country.

I quickly followed Bob to Guam. My son was born there. We hiked and snorkeled the entire island. We met friends for life who joined us on these adventures. Upon completion of Bob's military service, we returned to northern Iowa where Bob began building houses. Thankfully, Cleo convinced Bob to attend college on the GI Bill in Mankato, MN. During this time, two daughters were born.

With an engineering degree in hand, a new home and job, we settled in Mankato. The desire to travel was still strong. Money was tight and tent camping with three small children was difficult, so we built a small wood camper. We joined friends in travels throughout the Midwest and to local lakes most weekends. Travel with our children continued to be important. As they grew, we focused on areas of the country they were learning about in school.

We moved south away from cold weather to Indiana and then South Carolina. As the children started to finish high school, I received my Real Estate License and did extremely well. This job takes up a lot of your life and the customer demands are high. Both of our careers limited leisure travel, so I started to take annual hiking trips with Cleo and two friends to National Parks.

This time was "me" time, full of laughter and so important to reducing stress levels. I loved my time with these girls. The trips fulfilled my need for travel and learning about new areas of this vast and unique country.

During our trip to Alaska I realized something was wrong with my balance and stamina during a glacier hike. I could not finish it and had to sit and wait for the group to return. I saw a doctor when I got home. After much testing with many doctors, I was diagnosed with Parkinson's disease. This was the end of my hiking adventures.

I enjoyed the future trips vicariously through the shared Happy Hikers pictures and videos. I watched them over and over again. When my oldest daughter, Laurie, joined the group we would share her experiences each year. The ability to participate in this way was critical when trapped in a body that no longer would allow me to join the adventures. I was gifted with the trail name "Womanwithspirit" by the Happy Hikers.

—As told to Laurie Chandley

Cleo Simon

(Runningbehind)

I was born a farmer's daughter in the small town of Freeborn, Minnesota, the youngest of two sisters and one brother. From the time I could walk I wanted to be outside, and from the time I could talk I begged for a horse. For my sixth birthday I received a Shetland pony. I named her Penny and for the next seven years we were inseparable friends. I had a wonderful family, friends, my pony, and a whole countryside for riding. Life was good.

I spent my youth finding fun with Judy and Gloria, my two cousins, and sister, Maurene. She was six years older, but Maurene was always ready for an escapade and took us swimming and sledding often.

I graduated from high school in 1959 and with my best friend, Diann, enrolled in college. We took every class together, and helped each other study. I graduated in 1963 with a degree in elementary education and accepted a two year position on the island of Guam.

Once settled on the island, I was thrilled to find eight other newly graduated teachers from the Midwest. We lived in the same compound and bonded immediately. We called ourselves the "Go Group of Guam." We soon met a teacher from Guam named Doris Perez (Graham) and she also became part of our adventurous group. We explored every inch of that beautiful island together, became avid snorkelers, hiked Mt. Lam Lam, the tallest mountain in the world, and swam over the Mariana's Trench, the deepest spot in the ocean.

During the first summer on Guam, the Go Group took a monthlong tour of Japan, Hong Kong, Taiwan, and the Philippines. It was during this summer that I met a sailor named Ed Simon.

After completing my contract in 1965, I returned to the states via Australia, New Zealand and New Guinea. I taught for one year in Hawaii, sharing an apartment with Doris while Ed was in Viet Nam. We were married in Niceville, Florida, in 1966.

With service completed we moved to Punta Gorda, Florida, in 1973. While there I taught and Ed operated our tennis club. For the next thirty years we worked hard, played lots of tennis, went kayaking, motorcycling and enjoyed the west coast beaches.

While in Punta Gorda, two tennis club members and I found we had the same adventurous spirit. With Betsy as our mountain climbing motivator, Nancy as our organizer, and my sister Maurene and me making it a foursome, the Happy Hikers began their adventures. For one week every year, I am totally a free spirit, no responsibilities, except to delight in the uniqueness of each friend and to savor the wonders of nature while hiking. It is a "Peter Pan" week that fills my soul, leaving me refreshed and knowing "Life is Good."

Catherine Terburgh

(Wisdomwalk)

 I grew up in rural Michigan near lakes and thick lush hardwood forests where I fell in love with nature and outdoor experiences. My spiritual life really began as a young child when I experienced an awakening to the beauty and grandeur of nature under a large oak tree near my home in Michigan. This experience filled me with an awareness and awe of the divine in all things. From there I was called to a life filled with spending time in nature, meditation, prayer and service. As a teenager, I felt that becoming a nun was my path to fulfilling this passion.

While living in Colorado, I learned to hike and backpack in the Sangre de Cristo Mountains and along the Continental Divide. I was certified as a Wilderness Educator through the Alaska program of Wilderness Education Association designed by Paul Petzold, well known for establishing the National Outdoor Leadership School (NOLS).

Hiking the wilderness areas, mountains, glaciers and kayaking the waters of the Bay spurred me on to continue exploring the wild outdoors in the Rocky Mountains, Canada, White Mountains of New Hampshire, Vermont, Maine and Tibet. For my 50th birthday, I hiked the Grand Canyon Rim to Rim.

I finished my Masters in Education and then a Masters in Nursing and worked as a Family Nurse Practitioner, starting my profession providing primary and urgent care for the Seminole

Indian Tribe at their most remote clinic in the Everglades.

While there, my husband and I spent our free time kayaking and exploring the rivers, oldest canals, and the Wilderness Waterway which is considered the most remote and wild paddling trail in Florida. We joined the Main Island Trail Association as charter members.

After we moved to the state of Washington, I began hiking with the group of women named Happy Hikers. I am now retired, but continue part time as an integrative nurse wellness coach to help others enhance health and well-being through behavioral and lifestyle change, preventative care, wellness promotion, and integrative holistic therapies. Hiking with the women of the Happy Hikers has been a unique and fun filled addition to my hiking life.

Acknowledgments

This was a fun book for us to write about our travels. We fortunately had each other to nudge and critique through countless drafts and chapter rewrites. Each of us had a special niche where we could make the process grow and work. It was a dream to get our adventures in a book and like ascending a mountain we inched along little by little. We met many interesting people throughout our journeys who encouraged us in writing our travelogue. Of course, we can not leave out our buddies Dictionary, Thesaurus and Spell check that soon became our trusty side kicks.

We are most grateful for the thoughtful support of our editor, John Prince of Hallard Press who sensitively directed us on straighter courses then we might have chosen. Also our fellow Happy Hiker, Catherine Terburgh, who was not able to write a chapter while selling her house and moving, but still shared her expert contributions and memories. A big thanks goes to family and friends for their patience, helpfulness and willingness to lend their special talents with us. And thank you our readers, for letting us share our adventures one more time.

Cleo's Rules For A Perfect Trip

1. Never travel after dark.
2. Always get to the motel early.
3. Use the buddy system at all times.
4. Always buy good hiking boots.
5. Never forget your poncho.
6. Lunch is always the same:
     Raisins
     Granola Bars
     Bananas
     Anything with fiber.
7. If trip is more than 7 days bring 2
   sleeping outfits.
8. Recheck your packing checklist.
9. Always ride the local trolley.
10. Never listen to Cleo.

Made in the USA
Monee, IL
06 December 2020